Magical Gardens

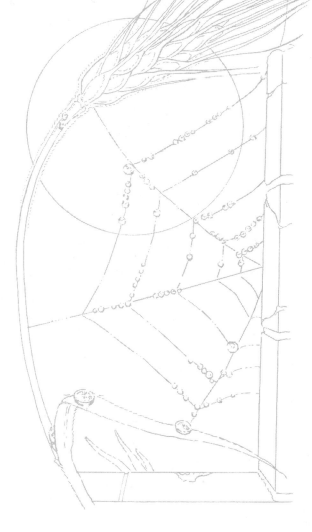

Cultivating Soil & Spirit

About the Author

One of the leaders of the contemporary earth-spirituality movement, Patricia Monaghan has spent more than twenty years researching and writing about alternative visions of the earth. Raised in Alaska, where much of her family still lives, she considers herself blessed to have learned the ecology of the taiga, the subarctic forest, in her youth. She was a writer and reporter on science- and energy-related issues before turning her attention to the impact of mythic structures on our everyday lives.

The worldwide vision of the earth as feminine—as a goddess, called Gaia by the Greeks—led her to recognize the connection between ecological damage and the oppression of the feminine in Western society. Much of her work since that time has explored the question of the role of feminine power in our world in an inclusive and multicultural way.

An avid traveler, Patricia has researched earth spirituality and goddess worship on three continents. She has traveled widely in Europe, especially in Ireland. She holds dual US/Irish citizenship and has edited two anthologies of contemporary Irish-American writing.

Patricia is a member of the resident faculty at DePaul University's School for New Learning in Chicago, where she teaches science and literature. Visit her online at www.patricia-monaghan.com.

Magical Gardens
Cultivating Soil & Spirit

Patricia Monaghan
Foreword by John Dromgoole

15th Anniversary Edition

Llewellyn Publications
WOODBURY, MINNESOTA

Book design: Rebecca Zins
Cover design: Adrienne W. Zimiga
Cover and interior floral ornament: www.istockphoto.com/Mehmet Ali Cida
Cover female sculpture: www.istockphoto.com/Hsing-Wen Hsu
Illustrations: Carrie Westfall

Llewellyn is a registered trademark of Llewellyn Worldwide Ltd.

ISBN 978-0-7387-3192-6

Llewellyn Publications
A Division of Llewellyn Worldwide Ltd.
2143 Wooddale Drive
Woodbury, MN 55125-2989

Printed in the United States of America

Other Books by Patricia Monaghan

The Goddess Path
(Llewellyn, 1999)

The Goddess Companion
(Llewellyn, 1999)

The Red-Haired Girl from the Bog
(New World Library, 2004)

The Encyclopedia of Celtic Mythology and Folklore
(Checkmark Books, 2008)

Contents

Chapter One
Myth, Mulch, and Marigolds   1

• • • • • •

Chapter Six
In Gaia's Name   211

• • • • • •

The Book of Gardens

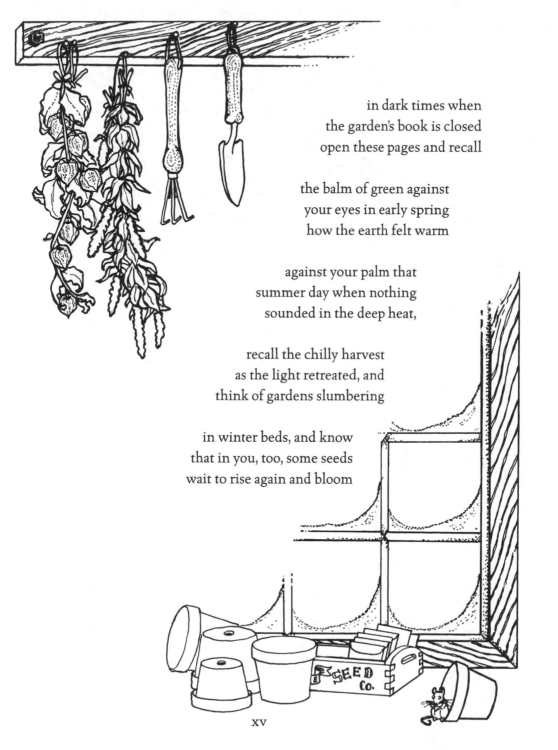

in dark times when
the garden's book is closed
open these pages and recall

the balm of green against
your eyes in early spring
how the earth felt warm

against your palm that
summer day when nothing
sounded in the deep heat,

recall the chilly harvest
as the light retreated, and
think of gardens slumbering

in winter beds, and know
that in you, too, some seeds
wait to rise again and bloom

Foreword

One night while out in my garden, I asked, "Spirit, what makes it grow so well?" When the answer came to me, it wasn't compost or organic fertilizers—it was love. When visitors come all day long, they admire it and say how lovely it is. I realize that love plays a huge role in the beauty and success of my garden. Love grows the prettiest, most spirit-filled gardens of them all. Ceremony is also an essential part of garden success. Read *Magical Gardens* and you'll know what I mean.

Patricia Monaghan has done a fantastic job of combining two things that are very dear to me: gardening and spirituality. Many gardeners enjoy the spiritual effects of gardening but don't really understand what they are experiencing. Patricia embraces gardening as prayer and celebration. The scope of information Patricia presents about the many styles of magical gardens that exist in our world is impressive. She tells incredible stories. In addition to Patricia's strong spiritual guidance, she teaches horticulture and garden design. As a shamanic practitioner and a gardener, I always keep *Magical Gardens* nearby for inspiration and direction. There is a true, heartfelt, spirit-filled presence in this book.

As Patricia writes, "If every garden is magic, then every gardener is by definition a magician."

I hope you enjoy reading this book, and go work some magic in your own garden!

John Lee Dromgoole
The Natural Gardener (Austin, Texas)
NATURALGARDENERAUSTIN.COM

Preface
to the Fifteenth Anniversary Edition

Every year since this book was first published, more Americans have embraced gardening. In pots on an urban patio, in suburban yards, or on rural acreage, they plant flowering shrubs and perennials, nurture tomatoes, and set out annual flowers. Whether these gardeners aim for fragrant bouquets on the mantle or a fabulous meal on the deck, all receive a common gift: an awakening of spiritual connection to the earth.

They may use different words to describe this blessing. They may say that gardening relaxes them or that tending the soil is a form of meditation. They may talk about the aesthetic beauty they find in leaf and flower. They may describe the sensory pleasures of taste, fragrance, color. All are different ways to acknowledge the transformative power of planting, tending, and harvesting, whereby gardener and earth co-create beauty and sustenance from the simplest of materials—from seed and soil, rain and sunshine.

And one of those creations is the gardener, who goes out to the garden with a worried frown and returns with dirty fingernails, a smile, and a lightened heart. Gardening roots the gardener in the present moment, with its specific mix of sun and shade, of growth and death, of beauty and frustration. It roots us as well in the history of humanity's search for a meaningful relationship with the earth that sustains us. What could be more spiritual than that?

At the same time as people are finding their way back to the garden for personal reasons, social and global reasons to garden have become more significant. Gardeners have been among the first to document the impact of climate change, as we notice beloved trees and plants affected by extreme weather or find ourselves suddenly able to grow a plant from another gardening zone. Whatever the cause of these shifts in climate, gardeners who pay attention to their land notice, and we are concerned. But gardeners and farmers, too, can aid in improving conditions by being aware of how our choices impact the soil, water, and air we share with our gardens and with every other living being.

Gardening reminds us daily of time's passing. In spring, a single kernel of corn goes into the ground. By July, it's knee-high. By late summer, its tassels wave in the breeze and its ears swell on the stalks. In late fall, the same stalks stand golden-beige in the chilling air. For those of us who plant trees, the visual yardstick of years can be even more dramatic. A two-foot-tall magnolia tree I planted fifteen years ago now towers over my head. Even the slow-growing beech I planted only seven years ago stretches above me now.

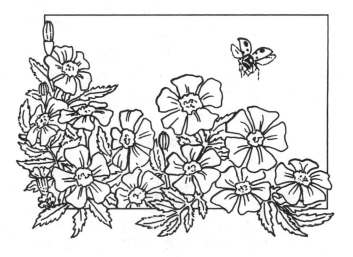

Just as dramatically, the world has changed since 1997. I wrote this book when Princess Diana was alive, when *Katrina* referred to a European rock group, when 911 meant nothing more than an emergency phone number. For most people, one of the most significant differences between then and now is the omnipresence of the Internet. I first composed this book on floppy discs, relying on books and catalogs for research because most nurseries did not yet have websites. I have been pleased, in doing this revision, to find that almost all of the plants originally used in the garden designs remain available. A few have gone out of circulation and have been replaced by similar varieties.

But more importantly, research has been made easier, because now a flick of the fingers gets you anywhere in the world of gardening. Thousands of seed and plant companies now advertise their wares online, and thousands of individuals and organizations offer their expertise on websites and blogs. The amount of information can be overwhelming, but if you know where and how to look, you can answer any question, find any plant or seed, and connect with communities of like-minded gardeners. Yet the grounding, glorious labor of gardening remains the same, even if the preparatory tasks are made easier by access.

Among the changes in this edition are two expansions: ideas for ritualizing our gardening lives and resources for gardeners. Regarding the first, the book remains unchanged in not offering cookie-cutter formulae or prewritten spells. Just as no gardens can be the same even if they are similar in zone, plant selection, and cultivation techniques, so no two gardeners are identical in their spiritual needs. Thus this book offers general outlines and suggestions for connecting the gardener's spirit with the spirit of the garden, so that you can create your own special and site-specific celebrations.

Another change is the great expansion of the resources section of the book, which now includes not only the sources for the myths and prayers but also a comprehensive list of nurseries that specialize in the kinds of plants used in the sample gardens. In chapter 5, a short section on exemplary magical and spiritual gardens offers additional inspiration beyond the garden patterns offered here.

My own life has undergone changes in the decade and a half since I first wrote *Magical Gardens*. I now spend weekends tending a farm in Wisconsin, creating a place where my husband and I will eventually live full time. Creating a self-sustaining homestead with an orchard, a vineyard, and vegetable fields has been at the forefront of our plans, but we also build magical gardens, small and large, on our land in Black Earth. None of them are exactly like the gardens described in this book, because any garden idea has to be brought down to earth—literally grounded in a specific place with its specific demands and challenges. But, as our farm project began after this book was written, some of our gardens are based on these plans, altered to fit the chosen sites.

The first project we started remains many years from completion: concentric circles of trees that represent the letters in the ancient Celtic tree alphabet—birch, oak, beech, rowan, and dozens more. Because we planted tiny saplings, it has taken many years to see the pattern of the sacred grove emerge. For years we have protected the trees in winter with deer fences, but some are finally now tall enough to outpace the nibbling neighbors. Soon we plan to label each tree with the ogham letter it represents, as well as its name in Irish and in English. For now, we show visitors a chart showing what tree is where.

Next came the fulfillment of a long-held dream. I had always wanted a formal herb garden, and an area in front of the house festooned with a dead crabapple was the perfect location. Tearing out the roots of the crabapple, leveling the ground, enriching the appallingly hard clay soil, and creating a Celtic cross centered on a stone birdbath took the better part of a summer. I confess it seemed an almost-impossible dream when we built that garden, but now as we pick peaches and pears from the corner trees and nip culinary herbs for eight months of the year, I am glad we put forth the effort. And in winter, as I watch the birds at the feeders around the garden, I am glad once again.

Other gardens followed: a tiny Kuan-Yin garden near the steps to the patio, a Zen garden (and pet graveyard), a spring garden of bulbs, a mailbox garden of shade perennials. Five years ago we started burning the prairie across from the house and were inspired to carve a Brigit's cross into the prairie grasses—so huge it can be seen from the air. We cleared debris from an old pine grove and placed furniture there to create the Pine Chapel. We cleared brush from around an old wildling apple and found that it rested against a snakelike, huge cottonwood root, inspiring us to name the clearing Eve's Bower.

Not all our efforts have been successful—yet. The winter garden suffers from a dire need for soil amendment and so far has produced only a few scrawny plants. But it's located near the back door and may eventually reward our work with leeks and Brussels sprouts into the snowy months. A section reserved for a goddess garden just sits there, its weedy fringes reminding me of the need to plan and plant. No appropriate low branch has been found for the swing I want to hang on the edges of the woodland, though I keep staring at trees, hoping I've missed something. Some of these plans may be abandoned; some will come to ultimate fruition.

But then there are surprising and even sudden successes. Last year I realized we had built our fire circle near a small artificial pond, and I had an inspiration. We added a circle of summer-flowering perennials (to represent earth) and a circle of plant stands decorated with birds (indicating air) to create the Elements Garden. Later that summer we found, after clearing invasive honeysuckle from a butternut grove at the edge of the property, that we had created the perfect place for a Wind Chamber. Hung with wind chimes, this outdoor room is charming in summer and delightful when we snowshoe over to it on a sunny winter day.

There is no end to the work of gardening, nor to the magic it brings into my life. In fact, it is hard to know where one begins and the other leaves off. It is my fervent wish that each reader will find some of the joy and meaning in gardening that I have been blessed to find.

Introduction
Before There Were Gardens

Once upon a time, there were no gardens—not a single one in the whole green world.

There were plants, yes: big, stretching baobab trees and sturdy wild yams and grassy savannahs. Each day, the trees waved their leaves in the soft winds, the yams silently swelled into firm tubers beneath their leafy crowns, and the grasses nodded heavy heads under the bright sun. Each night, the plants breathed and slept and grew, green in the silver moonlight.

There were people, too, in that time before time. But only two: the first woman, Abuk, and her mate, Garang. They would become the ancestors of the Dinka people and of all people everywhere, but at this time they were alone—alone and hungry. They wandered through the green world listening to the hooting of monkeys and the distant roar of lions. They wandered through vine-hung forests and across golden plains, constantly moving and always, always hungry.

They were hungry because they did not realize plants are food. They passed under a ripening breadfruit tree and never knew they could mark it for later harvest. Yams were merely sprawling mats of green leaves to them; they knew nothing of the tasty orange meat beneath the soil. Atop the ripening grasses, these first people did not see the swelling seeds that could be ground into flour and baked into bread. And so they passed through the fertile, bearing land and felt the hollow pains of hunger, never knowing how close they were to sustenance.

Abuk and Garang believed that food came directly from the sky. Once each day the creator would appear, reaching down a cloudy hand to give them each a single grain of corn. These miniscule rations were barely enough to sustain life, certainly not enough to ease the pangs of hunger. Yet, not knowing any other way to feed themselves, Abuk and Garang walked aimlessly through the green hills and golden fields of earth.

Abuk and Garang had more in common with the plants than they knew, for both had been raised from seeds the creator had made. With a wave of his hand, the deity had made them: two tiny people, fully formed, sound asleep, each only the size of a large bean. He put them into a big pot of water where, throughout an eternal night, they swelled and swelled and swelled. By the time the creator took the lid off the pot, Abuk and Garang had swollen to adult size. He tipped the pot over and out they sloshed, waking in surprise to see the world around them.

It was this fresh, green world in which they wandered, dependent on their creator for every bite of food. Many years passed—if years can be said to pass in the timeless world in which the first couple dwelled. They grew neither thinner nor fatter. They did not sicken and die, nor did they grow and thrive. Abuk and her partner simply walked and felt their hunger.

Only when they slept did that hunger ease—but perhaps it did not ease so much as hide in their dreams. Once Abuk dreamed of a tiger who roared so loudly that she covered her ears. Its huge tongue lolled out of its mouth as it roared, again and again, right into her face. Startled into consciousness, she heard the rumbling of her stomach. Even sleep was no hiding place from hunger.

One night Abuk had a dream in which she was eating, eating, eating, eating. She seemed to go on eating forever. In the dream, her stomach was full—it pressed out from her hipbones like a little bowl, and it felt hard when she pushed upon it with her dream-hands. She had a feeling of utter peace, as though there was nothing in the world to worry her.

But when she woke and felt again the sharp pangs, Abuk grew angry. "Why do we not have more food?" she demanded of Garang. "We could eat *seven* grains of corn and not be satisfied!"

Garang put down his head and would not meet her eyes. He did not understand her anger, for although he too was starving, he did not think to question God. His head turned slightly away, Garang showed his disdain for Abuk's angry outburst.

"Fine!" she said. "Fine! Pretend you don't hear me! But I want to know why we aren't getting more food!"

She began to shout at the sky. "You! Up there! Why don't we have more food?" Garang looked away in embarrassment and fear. He had never imagined talking to God that way.

But Abuk kept on. "Don't pretend you're not there! Don't pretend you can't hear us! *We want more food!*"

God answered.

But it was not words with which he answered. A deafening silence surrounded Abuk and Garang. It went on for many moments. No birds sang, no lions roared. There was no movement anywhere in the world. It was as though everything had become frozen, or died, or turned to stone.

Garang began to shake with fear. The world—their world—had always been a noisy one, filled with the sounds of animals and plants and wind and water. In the sudden stillness, the only sound was the angry slap of Abuk's hand on her naked thigh.

"Don't try to frighten me!" she yelled into the awful silence. "I am telling you *we want food!*" But no answer came, only silence.

Abuk put her hands on her hips. She had never asked for anything before, but now she felt fierce resolve burning in her breast. Somewhere, she knew, God was looking down at her. She wanted to be certain that he saw her as adamant and firm in her resolve to be fully fed.

Out of the corner of her eye, Abuk saw a sudden, slight movement. At the same instant, she heard a sound like sighing. She followed the sound with her eyes and saw a stalk of grass swaying slightly, as though signaling her.

Pulled by the grass's sudden motion, Abuk walked over to it. In the silence and stillness of that timeless moment, she saw—really saw, for the first time—the grass. She saw how the thin stalk curved gracefully downward, pulled earthward by the weight of its seed head. She saw a seed detach itself and float away, borne on its tiny filament sail. She saw the seed glide to earth and plant itself there, saw it sprout, saw it blossom and go to seed once more. A whole season's growth she saw in that endless moment.

And suddenly Abuk knew what she needed to do.

She walked closer to that stalk of grass and, holding its base with one hand, pulled the other—hard!—through the seeds. They fell off in her fist. When she opened her hand, there lay more seeds than God had given her in a month. Tentatively she reached out two fingers and picked up a seed. Placing it in her mouth, she bit it sharply. It filled her mouth with sour sweetness. She ate another, and another, and another. She ate more than the seven she had once imagined would be enough. She reached out and picked more, more, more, and ate until her stomach was tight and she felt a sleepy fullness.

When she looked up, she saw Garang a few feet away, filling his hands and his mouth with seeds. And then she noticed that sound and motion had returned to the world. The heavens were smiling with sun. God, she realized, had given her the answer to her need. All those endless years of wandering could have ended sooner had she only realized that her hunger was a sign that it was time to ask for more.

And so Abuk learned how to feed herself and the many children who grew about her in the following years. Together they tended the plants that gave them sustenance. The plants themselves taught Abuk where they liked to grow and what conditions they demanded. As she learned what they wished to teach, she grew to love and respect the creatures that gave her their seeds, their stalks, their very selves so that she might live and thrive.

The plants respected and loved Abuk as well. When, aged and bent, Abuk knew the time had come to die, she had no fear. She went back to the place where she had first seen the waving grasses and lay down on the earth to die. The earth opened beneath her and, as she sank into the soil, the grasses waved a slow and sad farewell to Abuk, the first woman, mother of all gardens.

One
Myth, Mulch, and Marigolds

Bloudewedd

From mountain primrose, from rose and thorn,

from nettle blossoms that bloom in shade,

from gorse and thistle I am made,

from lady's mantle I was born.

Nine flowers gave nine powers, nine trees,

and nine more herbs are what formed me.

I am called Bloudewedd.

Earth and magic are in my blood.

• • • • • •

Welsh song to the flower goddess

All gardens are magical.

Abuk, mother goddess of the African Dinka people, lived in a magical garden where plants told her how to tend and harvest them. The Polynesian Hainuwele, whom we will encounter in a later chapter, was a magical being who brought life to her people's gardens. And in the Western tradition, the ancestral mother Eve lived in a garden called Eden or Paradise.

Magical gardens exist in many mythologies, but they exist in our world too. That garden outside your door—isn't it a magical one? It might look ordinary, with its weeds and bugs, its patches of poor soil and points of dense, dry shade. It hardly seems magical on those early summer days when the smallest weed seems twice the size of the biggest vegetable. It can seem like the farthest thing from magic, the plot of ground that is simultaneously too small for our dreams and too large for our energies.

Yet that garden—that patch or acre or estate, that land where you encounter the primal forces of nature—is magic. What gardener has not felt the subtle attunement of self to universe that occurs when, on a late winter day no less blustery than the one before, a garden cries out for that great act of faith, planting—and then, within days, spring breaks like a sudden warm wave? What gardener has not recognized the combination of intent and surprise that comes of finding a self-sown bed of bright annuals across the garden from their parents? What gardener has not felt the subtle, slow shift as the inner world aligns itself with the outer, occurring in the midst of even the humblest task, thinning carrots or mulching melons?

Magic is the transformation of the ordinary into the extraordinary. And what better demonstration can we find than the rose unfurling its changeful beauties, the daffodil illuminating the spring sunshine, the daisy bobbing in a summer breeze?

Gardeners are weavers of magic. A seed is planted. Some months later, a tall plant waves its flowers or dangles its fruit before us. No matter how many years a gardener has worked the soil, the ongoing miracle of vegetative life always seems magical. Take carrots. Those tiny seeds! They are so miniscule that our fingers are too clumsy to hold them individually. Yet in just a few months, these black dots put out tall plumed heads and build tough orange roots a half-foot long. When a carrot comes to the table, that miracle comes with it. When we eat, we take communion

with soil and water and air. Our bodies take nourishment and then—invisibly and magically—transform the flesh of the carrot into human flesh, thought, energy, and love.

Magic is not confined to the vegetable garden. We are nourished as well by the visual beauty of flowers and shrubs. Throughout the year, a garden lavishes its gifts upon our senses. Winter trees trace their lacy outlines on the gray sky. Then burgeoning begins, and crocuses peep from melting snow. Soon peonies fling themselves upon the ground, glorious blooms too heavy even for their sturdy stalks. Shrubs bedeck themselves with flowers and blow heady fragrances into the air. Daisies banner the garden with color. Roses festoon fences and arbors with gorgeous crimsons, clear pinks, pristine whites. Asters shine like miniature stars, and the pompoms of chrysanthemums cheer us into fall. Then trees blanket themselves in one last dance of color before winter comes again to garden and to gardener.

For thousands of years people have cooperated with earth's transformations by cultivating plants near their homes, for that is the essence of the garden: whether composed of herbs or roses, grasses or vines, a garden is nearby nature. It may become weedy and wild when we momentarily turn our backs, but it is not wilderness. It is the place where nature's fecund beauty meets our energy and our desire, a threshold between wildness and the enclosures we need for comfort and protection.

Magic occurs when nature's fecund beauty meets our energy and our desire. In the garden we corral nature's blossoms and fruits for our pleasure and nourishment. She responds on her own terms, giving some gifts we never thought to seek and withholding others we crave. Nature and the gardener bend and sway in a dance that, for all its various forms, is ultimately the same in bee-loud gardens everywhere.

If every garden is magic, then every gardener is by definition a magician. Some are unconscious of this aspect of gardening, even unwilling to define their activity in this way; they think of gardening merely as an aesthetic pleasure or as good exercise. Others, however, eagerly embrace the magical aspects of gardening. For such gardeners, gardening is a life-enhancing ritual that can be connected consciously with all other such rituals. For the magical gardener, dream and poem and dance are as much a part of the garden as fertilizer and seed. So are myth and legend and story, ancient rituals, old songs and prayers, and the folkways of ancestors.

The magical gardener is never entirely alone in the garden, for goddesses and gods, elves and devas—powers of life and growth, however they are named—are there as well. They may make their presence known through tantalizing and playful occurrences, or they may remain watchful and hidden. The magical gardener never doubts that there are powers to be encountered just outside the back door and listens for the spiritual messages gardens offer. Magical gardening means consciously engaging in the cosmic dance, consciously holding out a hand to the earth, consciously forging connection.

MYTH, MULCH, AND MARIGOLDS

Magical gardening is for anyone who desires a soulful approach to tending the flowers, lawns, shrubs, trees, and vegetables that fill nearby land. You may already practice an earth-based or magical tradition. If you do, you'll find ideas in this book for incorporating the garden into your ritual and spiritual life. If you practice another religion, or none, you'll find this book useful in discovering connections between spirit and body, between land and soul. For the magical garden is not a location for a specific kind of religious celebration. It is an acre of our hearts wherein we learn to enrich both ourselves and our earthly abode with grace, joy, and genuine love.

There are three components to magical gardening: becoming aware of traditions and narratives that hold insights into the connection between self and earth; becoming conscious of the earth's special needs, the better to craft a connection to her; and becoming knowledgeable about specific plants and techniques that lead to gardening success—myth, mulch, and marigolds, respectively. In this chapter we will examine each in turn. In following chapters we will explore the connections among them. Finally, we'll look at specific garden plans that incorporate the principles of magical gardening to create spaces that enrich our senses, engage our imagination, and encourage the connection of self and spirit.

Myth:
Stories That Nourish and Bloom

Once upon a time, in a garden…

How many myths and legends begin that way? Dozens, scores, hundreds, for the garden is one of the great archetypal settings for stories of spiritual power. Western civilization's major myth begins with the image of Eden, a place where humans and animals live in timeless, carefree comfort. There, a divine gardener provides all manner of tasty fruits and foods for Eden's occupants, who graze through the garden, never having to stoop to plant or labor to harvest. Untimely weather never destroys seedlings, nor does drought ever wither Adam and Eve's dinner. And although Genesis does not provide exact pest-control information, it does not appear that slugs ever ravish its crops.

Into this idyll, scripture tells us, comes a devilish serpent who tempts our ancestors to eat from the one forbidden tree. Having succumbed to the snake's blandishments, humans are cast out of Eden, forced thereafter to toil and sweat, to plant and cultivate and harvest. This world, then—our culture's major myth tells us—is a failed copy of a glorious original. The garden of Eden, invisibly tended and watered, was a place in which all was predictably beautiful and perfect. Our world may be beautiful, its fruits sweet and its flowers fragrant, but somewhere beyond time real beauty, real sweetness, real fragrance has been lost because of human hunger.

How different is the myth of Abuk, whose acknowledgment of her hunger led to human salvation. Like other important myths, the story of Abuk, as told by the Dinka people of the upper Nile, describes the emergence of agriculture, that point in human history when we began to cultivate plants. Although it is common to think of preagricultural people as living primarily on hunted meat, scholars theorize that 75 to 80 percent of the daily food supply was provided by women gathering plants. To provide enough for oneself and one's growing family meant an intimate knowledge of the plants of an area—when they were best to eat, what preparation was necessary, and, most importantly, what parts of the plants were poisonous or toxic. From there, it is thought, women began to cultivate plants by spreading seeds of especially tasty or productive varieties. This agricultural revolution some five thousand years ago was the most significant change in human

history, leading to the establishment of permanent settlements, the better to be near the productive fields.

When markets are filled with strawberries in December and squash in July, it is easy to forget that in the past we ate what was fresh in summer and devoured our stored seeds and tubers in winter. When we grew sick, wise women healed us with herbs. Women processed vegetable fibers into cloth and baskets to clothe their families and provide storage. We knew the names of the trees that shaded our villages and the plants that grew in the fields because without that knowledge we would not survive.

Today such intimate knowledge of the plants that surround us is rare, but it was common to those who honored the Greek corn goddess Demeter, the South American manioc mother Nugkui, or the Russian grain goddess Zemyna. Yet even if we don't recognize the names of plants, we can appreciate their beauty and, if they are edible, their taste and nourishment. We are never far from realizing the magic in the garden. We just have to take time to look, touch, taste, and smell, and the magic begins.

The myths and legends that speak to the magical gardener's soul have their origin in those primal sensory encounters with the earth's soil and vegetation. And the ancient stories tell of a different relationship than the story of Eve's punishment for tasting the fruits of Eden.

Not that Eden doesn't hold a seductive appeal. Every winter it tempts the mind's eye. This year, the Eden vision promises, the peas will clamber up their little fences without fail, every tomato will ripen, every carrot will thicken without growing woody or splitting, and not a single overlooked zucchini will swell to cannon size beneath its sheltering leaves. In the flower border, the alyssum will spread evenly across the edge, the rose leaves will flourish unspotted, and—most importantly— no weeds will outstrip the seeded annuals.

This imagined Eden is the seedbed of the real garden in which rains cause seedlings to damp off, roses are attacked by rust, and volunteer yarrow runs amok in the perennial bed. Real weeds display their astonishing vigor, perseverance, and fecundity. Real squirrels eat the strawberries, real crows peck out the beans, real deer sneak out of the woods at twilight to nibble the apples. The magical gardener looks, listens, learns—and continues gardening, for it is in this tension between the dreamed-of Eden and the changing, challenging real garden that we find our greatest lessons.

Even if Eden were possible, it would not last long. Imagine a moment of garden perfection: not a weed can be seen; every leaf is whole and unblemished; the flowers hold brilliant blossoms out for our delight. But come back the next day: flowers need deadheading, trees cry out for pruning, bushes stretch out ungainly shoots, and perennials crowd themselves beyond flowering.

Perfection is an instant in the garden's life. And so the gardener once again joins the dance of planting, tending, and harvesting.

Although Eden is held up as an image of gardening perfection, the magical gardener would not, in fact, feel comfortable in such a place. For what gives gardening its pleasure as well as its spiritual meaning is the dance between imagined perfection and hard-won reality. The myth of Eden presents a distinctly unmagical garden, but myths and legends of other cultures speak to the magical gardener's soul.

Ancient and tribal people created narratives that revealed how plant and human life are connected. Often in these tales the earth is female—sometimes a mother, sometimes a splendid, fair daughter. The Greeks sing of Demeter, searching weeping through the world for lost Persephone and spreading flowers across the land when she returns. The Cherokee tell of Selu, the old corn mother who gives of herself that her children may eat. The Japanese relate a similar tale of the goddess Ukemochi, whose body decays into all the foods we need to survive.

Although such myths often picture the earth as feminine, we can also find stories that define the earth as masculine. Some cultures, like the Egyptian, personify the earth as a god; in Africa, stone monuments called "earth penises" show the earth as a virile force. Also common was the perception that, even while the earth was feminine, the vegetation covering her was masculine. Thus Attis, Adonis, and other dying-and-reviving gods of the ancient eastern Mediterranean were celebrated with rituals and symbols emphasizing their connection to plant life—the planting of short-lived Adonis gardens, the harvesting of pine trees to represent Attis.

No single worldwide myth represents all that we know about the earth. Rather, myriad, complex spiritual realities perceived by our forebears have been wrought into dozens of beautiful (although sometimes terrifying) stories. The earth is no more feminine than it is masculine. Similarly, the earth is not only generous and kindly. It can also be pictured as proud, wanton, withholding—and sometimes as all of these at once.

The magical gardener learns these stories. On dark winter nights it is not enough just to read seed catalogs and sketch color diagrams. A magical gardener knows that it's not enough to study Latin nomenclature while knowing nothing of Roman religion, with its wild-strawberry goddess Venus and its spring rituals of bean tossing. To plant dusty miller without recognizing it as a plant named for the wildwood goddess Artemis is unthinkable to such a gardener. The lore and legend of each plant is as important to the magical gardener as its climatic suitability, its form, its color. It is this attention to the archetypal, the symbolic, the mythic, that distinguishes the magical gardener.

Mulch:
Actions That Nurture the Earth

Gardens provide joy and nourishment for us. What do we give back?

A one-sided relationship with the earth is impossible for the magical gardener. Even if, in the beginning, we are only interested in what we get from the garden, within a few growing seasons we are forced to become more balanced. For what garden plot will go on yielding, year after year, without irrigation, without cultivation, without the soil being nourished in return?

Much of a gardener's work revolves around nurturing the soil. From the first spadeful of dirt turned over during spring cultivation to the removal of pest-harboring leaf litter in late fall, the garden's year is organized around earth-sustaining tasks. It is certainly possible to take shortcuts—to bloat plants with chemical fertilizers, to poison the garden in attempts at pest control. The well-meaning gardener may employ such techniques ignorantly in the beginning or in desperation later. But shortcuts have a price, whether paid onsite or downriver, whether paid in this growing season or another. The magical gardener soon realizes that the earth is not a servant—not even an employee. The earth is a parent, a child, a lover. The earth, seen as a person, is one who asks for an equal relationship, giving and receiving. Generous as it may be, the earth needs for us to be just as generous in return.

One of the true joys of gardening is intimacy with a specific piece of land. Thus, although the mythic paradigm most often used in speaking of Gaia is a maternal one (Mother Earth), the actual experience of gardening is more like being in love. Not, perhaps, like falling in love, although the first sight of a fertile new garden plot can evoke something like infatuation. No: to garden is to make love last, to learn by heart the land's tiny quirks and peculiarities, to relish the predictable moments of joy and to delight in the unpredictable ones, to soothe hurts and to embrace limitations. One who has learned to garden has learned to love; one who knows about love can certainly learn to garden. And if you are not yet a lover of earth or of others, becoming a gardener for more than one season will help you learn how to be one.

To love the earth, the gardener must nurture it. Left alone, the earth is self-renewing. In wilderness, the land does not call out for artificial irrigation or winter mulching. Ecosystems adapt to climate, birds and animals both devour and spread plants, and balance is maintained. That balance is not, however, always maintained gently. A harsh winter kills seedlings, fire levels an old-growth forest, drought parches a marsh. The balance is a rough one, in all meanings of that word, and it is maintained over years rather than single seasons.

But a garden is not wilderness. Where we create gardens, we change nature. The change begins with the building of our necessary shelters. Then we reach beyond the house to tame and settle the lands around us. We cut down trees that might fall on our homes. We plant a line of poplars to protect our homes from wind, or oaks to shade it. We sink a well, drawing out the invisible water that has fed deep-rooted plants, and splash it on shallow-rooted but cheery flowers. Altering nature's plan, we must then take responsibility to maintain the environment we have created. As the French author Antoine de Saint-Exupéry said, we become responsible for that which we tame.

One could easily, from this description, see the gardener as a consciousness separate from the vast mind of Gaia. Such a gardener would willfully impose on Gaia's order, creating an artificial one despite her, but no one is separate from the earth. It is just as possible to see the gardener—working in the hot sun, turning soil, casting seeds, harvesting and mulching—as earth's servant, and perhaps this vision is more accurate. Can we really be sure it is human arrogance that leads arctic gardeners to spend thousands of dollars to build greenhouses to nurture tomatoes, rather than the desire of the tomato family to travel? How can we be certain that a yearning desire for a rose garden *just there* is not the dream of the land itself, rather than one that is entirely the gardener's? For if the gardener is part of nature, not separate from her, then our work is an expression of the world itself.

Thus the second part of magical gardening is the nurturance of the earth that nurtures us. It is an ongoing university of mind, body, and spirit, wherein we let the earth teach us of her needs—and where, in meeting them, we learn to meet our own.

Marigolds:
Knowledge That Heals and Sustains

In Greek myth, Midas was a king so compulsively greedy that it was not enough for him to pile up all the gold in the land. One day, overcome with craving for the yellow metal, he prayed that everything he touched would be turned into gold. Granted that wish, Midas rushed about his palace in a frenzy, turning everything—from old dishpans to buzzing flies—into gold. Rounding a corner, Midas discovered his small daughter. Excited about his newfound power, Midas embraced her joyously.

The girl's warm flesh grew cold beneath his fingertips, and her smile stiffened. In an instant, the princess became a small gold statue, a look of baffled love still upon her face.

Happily for the king—and even more happily for the princess—his "Midas touch" was reversed. The child warmed and softened again as he kissed her back to life. Then the king rushed back through his palace, returning everything to its pre-golden state. Only a little flower, the marigold, was not quite restored: its blossoms remained colored brilliantly gold as a reminder to us all not to make Midas's mistake.

And what was that mistake? The story is usually viewed as a cautionary tale about greed: don't value money more than the tender embrace of loved ones, it warns. Don't settle for dead metal when you can enjoy the living presence of birds and flowers. Don't imagine that what can be bought will make you happier than what cannot.

Magical gardeners can glean even more meaning from this simple story, for the compulsion that Midas feels is a familiar one: to trade this mortal, ever-changing world for an immutable, even immortal, one. Yet the only real joy, as the king finds, is in those very temporal—and temporary—beings whom he earlier spurned. This is a lesson magical gardeners learn over and over: that we cannot cling to the beauties of our lives and our gardens, for part of beauty is transience. The flush of early season brilliance passes across the rose garden and fades. Autumn sweeps color across the trees, then fades. The glassy shine of icy lace on a winter's morning melts all too soon.

Gardening, as a spiritual discipline, forces us to live wholly in the present, to acknowledge each moment's special beauty and brevity. When we observe a bee alighting upon a perfectly formed sunflower, we can choose to ignore it and keep weeding or we can pause to attend to its passing glory. There is a part of each gardener pushing forward, calling us to plan, to labor, to produce. But there is another part that stops planning, laboring, producing—stops and holds still within an endless moment. If part of each gardener seeks to alter the landscape, another part simply loves this sensuous world while acknowledging its mortality.

Unlike Midas, gardeners do not seek to freeze this world into static perfection. Rather, they recognize where true gold is found. The Greeks called the goddess Aphrodite "the golden one" because of the way in which love transforms the beloved with radiant beauty. A similar radiance illuminates the garden when it is tended with love and deep care. Gardening stops us and holds us still within an endless moment.

Just as love among people is based on intimate knowledge, so it is for the gardener. While it is easy to be infatuated with the colors and fragrances of a plant whose name you do not know, real relationship is built upon knowledge: of a plant's preferred conditions for growth, its season of bloom, its history and lore. So the final part of magical gardening is understanding the individual plants that compose the garden as well as the design principles that join them into a complementary whole.

That marigold, for instance: it is a sun-loving annual of the genus *Tagetes*, named for the god Tages who taught the Etruscans how to find gold through divining. The plant has a long history of connection with gold; its common name derives from an early Christian practice of offering it in place of coins at Marian altars, hence

"Mary's gold." In Mexico, marigold is the most popular flower for decking altars on the Day of the Dead, November 2, for its golden bloom is thought to attract ancestors back to earth. In Nepal, at the festival of lights, Tihar (similar to the more widely known Hindu festival of Divali), dogs are festooned with marigolds and painted with a *tilika*, a "third eye" on the forehead. There the marigold is called the "hundred-leaved flower," a reference to its many petals.

Valued for its healing properties, the marigold has been used in many ways: as a garnish on broth to strengthen the heart, as an ointment for toothache, as a wart remover when mixed with wine. A favorite companion plant for many vegetables, it is believed to repel the parasitic worms called nematodes; its pungency is also said to repel four-legged pests like rabbits from devouring tasty greens like lettuce. Planting marigolds, the magical gardener attempts not only to find the appropriate placement in the garden but also to employ its history and lore in building and balancing the magical garden.

The plants that come to us bear encoded within them the history of the genus and species of which they are a part. We gardeners are just the latest representatives of the humans who have acknowledged, tended, or even tried to eliminate that plant's kin. We are not alone in the garden, even when we labor quietly at dawn in an apparently silent world. Around us are the ghosts of gardeners past, tending gardens past. We can connect with these early gardeners consciously through study and research. We can also, sometimes, feel their elusive presence when we move as they moved beneath the same sky that roofed their world. Just as in dreams we can encounter archetypal forces, so in the waking dream of the garden we can sense the power of the eons-old relationship between humanity and the plant kingdom. Through intimate knowledge of the plants and their needs, we forge the connection between our species and theirs.

Other gardeners, as well as books like this, will help you gain that intimate knowledge, which grows over many years. As those years pass, celebrate your deepening knowledge through ritual that uses the garden both to mark seasonal changes and the changes in your life. As the cycle of the garden's year meshes with the longer cycle of your growth, maturation, and decline, you will deepen your connection to the earth and the earth's other children.

Dark Woods and Primrose Paths

This book introduces you to some of the ways in which gardening is a form of magic. You may choose to define magic as ritual action taken to create change in the world, as a way of attuning oneself to cosmic forces, or even as a joyous and delightful sensual experience, as when we say of a splendid evening, "it was just magical!" Because magic cannot be dogmatically defined, neither can the magical garden. It is any garden that you, in consciousness and with intent, create for yourself and for your own healing.

It is not a garden without shadow, for darkness is part of life as well as dawn and bright midday. It is not a garden without weeds, for chaos is an omnipresent force in life and in the garden. Caring for such a garden is not an unmitigated joy, for there will be days of frustration as well as those of delight. But your magical garden will be a source of continuing inspiration for you. It will be one of your greatest teachers, showing you ways into spirit you had not previously seen and could not otherwise discern.

Two

Meditations, Dreams, and Rituals

Tellus Mater

Tellus, Holy Mother, source of nature,
you feed us while we live, you hold us when we die.
Everything comes from you, everything returns to you.
What else could we call you but Our Mother?
Even the gods call you that. Without you
there is nothing. Nothing can thrive, nothing can live
without your power. Queen and goddess, I invoke you:
you are all-powerful, and my needs are so small.
Give me what I ask, and in exchange, I will give you
my thanks, sincere and from my deepest heart.

• • • • • •

Roman prayer to the earth

Somewhere in the world at this moment, just as you read this, a community celebrates the miracles of garden and fertile field.

In Bali a procession of dancers in jewel-toned silks forms to dance in honor of Dewi Shri, the rice goddess. In Ireland picnickers stain their mouths with dark bilberries, not even aware that they celebrate a millennium-old rite in honor of Taillte, goddess of midsummer. In Oaxaca, in southern Mexico, enormous radishes carved into historical and religious dioramas line the poinsettia-garlanded square. There is not a day of the year when some community somewhere does not celebrate the divinities of planting, first fruits, or harvest.

In the United States we have no national religious ritual that reinforces awareness of our dependence on the garden's cycle, yet we gather to praise earth's bounty, especially in rural areas. We call these events state fairs or historical pageants or beauty contests, but Alice in Dairyland and Princess Kay of the Milky Way are only the most recent incarnations of a primal ritual in which a young woman represents the earth goddess herself, bestowing largesse upon her needy children.

Even urban families participate in the yearly cycle of food production and consumption. Instead of pouring milk into the first furrow, we barbecue on the deck for Memorial Day. Instead of offering first fruits, we eat sweet corn on the Fourth of July. And instead of cutting the carleen—the harvest's final sheaf of wheat or oats—we take a long first weekend in September, bidding farewell to the growing season even if we've never planted anything but a windowbox of geraniums.

In ancient times these rituals constituted part of an overarching religious understanding of the relationship between humans and the earth—one in which the many-named goddess and her consort were honored in rituals that enacted their mythology. Each spring in the ancient eastern Mediterranean, women planted tiny pots of quick-growing grasses that they tended and watered carefully. The grasses sprouted quickly but died within days. The women then ran through the streets or the fields, weeping loudly and tearing their veils in anguish. In this way they embodied the myth of the goddess (variously called Aphrodite, Ishtar, and Inanna) mourning her young lover (Adonis, Tammuz, or Dumuzi), bringing that timeless story into their present, into their homes and fields.

Similarly, the ancient Phrygians, who lived in what is now northern Turkey, cut down a pine tree, which they carried ceremoniously to a ritual site. There they

erected the little tree and danced around it. The festival, transported many centuries later to imperial Rome, represented the death and resurrection of the young god Attis, beloved of the mountain mother Cybele.

Often such festivals long outlasted the religious systems that gave rise to them. Today in County Kerry, in the far southwest of Ireland, an event called Puck Fair is, some claim, the oldest continually celebrated harvest festival in the world, dating back as long as two thousand years ago. There, wildly cheering revelers carry a goat through the town, hoisting it onto a platform after crowning it the harvest king. In ancient times, the connection of Panlike goat to harvest god would have been obvious to all, but now the fair is an occasion for merriment and flirtation, and few consciously honor the god incarnated, for those few days, in the little bearded Puck, who is finally released again to the wilds of the nearby mountains. What strange memories that Puck must carry back to the wild!

With no communally accepted myth to form a basis for our yearly rituals, contemporary gardeners create—whether consciously or not—their own private ones, events that both celebrate the garden's bounty and send out a prayer for another year of abundance. A family in Alaska burns off cleared brush before Hallowe'en trick-or-treating. A Midwestern gardener holds an annual garden party to show off the year's landscaping progress. A woman in California makes a special jam from the apricots her tree bears, gifting her friends in winter with the preserves of summer. Part of the pleasure each gardener experiences is in the establishment and maintenance of such ritualized prayers.

Ritual is a message from the conscious to the unconscious mind, just as dreams carry messages from unconsciousness to consciousness. Thus any action undertaken in a deliberate and prayerful way can become a ritual: setting your seeds, harvesting your first vegetable of the year (probably a radish!), putting the garden to sleep in the fall. Even without a conscious plan, the archetypal actions we take—clearing the land, tilling the soil, placing the seeds, cultivating, harvesting—are redolent with meaning. We do not have to be conscious of the deeper meanings of these actions for them to work upon our minds and souls.

Nor do we have to pray to a specific divinity as we garden, for gardening itself is a dance of prayer to the bountiful earth. The myths that inspired Mediterranean women to weep for Adonis, the ancient Irish beliefs that color the Puck Fair festivities—these sprang from the same source available to us today: the dreaming mind, wherein images and narratives are born. In learning magical gardening, it is important to connect with this inner source. Learning the myths and traditions of ancient times and other peoples is useful, but only insofar as they reflect our own inner landscapes. The first step in magical gardening is to examine our own personal mythology, our own connection to the dreamtime.

Simple Rituals of Mindfulness

Making our actions deliberate and conscious can intensify our spiritual connection to the land we cultivate, whether that be acres of mountain estate, borrowed land in a community plot, a patch of suburban lawn, or a couple of pots on a city balcony. We need not dress in embroidered cloaks and chant in ancient tongues over our gardens, for the true magic—the transformation of seed into flower into fruit—is the earth's. Rather, we should find ways of witnessing this transformation, of incorporating spiritual consciousness into each garden task.

Here are some examples of ways to do so:

- Provide food and especially water within the garden for wildlife, whether birds, small mammals, or larger animals.

- While weeding, acknowledge the lives we sacrifice for the food or beauty that will nourish us.

- Share the garden's bounty, whether through bouquets or through gifts of vegetables and fruit. Especially share the garden's bounty with those in need. (Some communities have food banks for small farmers and gardeners who wish to contribute to relief efforts, so that your seven extra tomatoes do not go to waste; consider organizing or cooperating with such an effort in your community.)

- Bring art into the garden, for art is one of the ways in which ritual finds an outlet. Make sculptures and birdhouses, paint or photograph flowers, sew flags and banners. Make twisted-twig tepees for beans and peas. Paint a welcome sign for the garden gate.

- Take a moment to hold seeds before planting, studying their wonderful smallness and their incredible potential for growth.

- Treat rake, hoe, and other tools as magical implements (and so they are!), handling them with respect and thanking them for their work for us.

- Store seeds from plants that have been successful in our garden, sharing the surplus each spring at a gardener's festival or donating them to a community garden.

- Make art out of the garden through dried bouquets, pressed flowers, honeyed preserves, and magnificent pies.

There are innumerable other ways of celebrating the garden cycle, and a creative consciousness will gradually unveil the ones most appropriate to your lifestyle and region. To become a true ritual, however, the act must be repeated regularly or annually. It needs to become part of your consciousness of gardening. Such private rituals may take years to develop and take root. They begin in meditation, move into creative action, and are sustained through faith and love.

To inspire you to create your own garden rituals, here are four meditations based on the year's gardening cycle. They represent a year of establishing a garden in a conscious and creative way. Each meditation includes suggestions for adapting it to later years' gardening endeavors. Do not think of them as something to be followed like a set of rules or laws. Rather, these offer a pattern for you to adapt to your own unique needs.

Winter:
Dreaming the Garden

All gardens begin in winter dreams.

The garden year begins with the arrival of the first seed catalog, its brilliantly toned pictures promising a perfect garden in a perfect summer. Ah, winter, that time of utter freedom, of reckless excess, of abandonment to the dreams of splendid gardens to come. Nothing is so hopeful as a gardener's plans in winter, when there is no chance of testing them against reality.

Yet any dream of the future has its roots in the past, and for a gardener, the past includes all the lost and abandoned gardens of other years, the ones that never lived up to their potential as well as the ones that flowered and fruited beyond our wildest winter dreams. To prepare for consecrating the spring garden, winter requires a ritual of farewell to all the gardens of the past.

Perhaps you recall a garden from childhood, abandoned when you left for college. Perhaps there was a garden you lost when a relationship ended. You moved to take a better job and left your garden behind. Or perhaps you have never gardened but remember the garden of a parent, neighbor, or friend. The first part of establishing a spiritual relationship with your current garden is the remembrance of, and possibly mourning for, the gardens you have left behind.

This meditation is best done privately in a journal or in your mind's eye. Perhaps you have a friend or two who would appreciate the opportunity to resanctify their gardens and their gardening selves. In that case, this meditation can form the basis of one or more exploratory conversations.

Begin by making a list of all the significant gardens of your life: yours, your family's, your friends'. Describe each of them. If you can, draw a picture or diagram of each. Of each of them, answer the following questions:

- What part of the garden did you love the most?

- What was the most frustrating part of the garden?

- What was the cycle of the garden's year? In what order were chores and tasks done or public and family events held?

- What personal relationships were connected with the garden? Did they change over the time of that garden?

- When and why did you leave the garden?

- If you were a plant or flower in the garden, what would you be? Why?

- How do you picture the garden looking today?

As you remember each garden, pay special attention to the feelings evoked. When you have finished with each garden, select one plant from that garden that was especially significant to you and that would grow in your new garden. As you plan your garden, keep this list handy.

The second part of this meditation is garden planning. Dozens of books are available that give useful information on garden design and plant adaptation. However, aesthetic considerations are not the only things at work when we design a garden. There is also our inner drive to adapt the landscape to truly represent the gardener. Thus, the second part of this meditation should be employed each year as you begin planning your summer's work in your garden.

It is easy to fall into one of two traps in garden planning. In the first, one adopts a style because it is popular, without considering whether it fits one's needs or lifestyle. One can hardly pick up a garden magazine without seeing a feature on a naturalistic garden, yet perhaps a Zen garden is more your style. The other trap is not to plan at all, relying either on already-established plantings or on haphazard seeding. But if the intent of gardening is to sing praises to the earth, and if that song is the unique worship of the individual gardener, then neither of these approaches is appropriate.

Rather, planning the garden should be undertaken as a meditative ritual. As with any ritual, it is important to set aside a place for it. Piles of seed catalogs on the desk, in the living room, on the counter—that hardly constitutes a gardening altar! Rather, designate a space in your home for garden planning, and consolidate all your materials within it. You'll need shelf space for books on design, history, and plant possibilities; a desk or table for creating potential plans; perhaps a computer if you wish to use its design tools; and some symbols of your garden, whether those be photographs or dried flowers.

You'll doubtless browse through seed catalogs and books in various spaces and at various times. They may find their way to bedside table, breakfast nook, bathroom, or study, but when the time comes for actual planning, use your designated space. Such space is a cue to the body-mind that imaginative doors should swing open readily.

Gardening experts agree that planning on paper is vital to the success of your garden, and many gardeners agree. Yet there are also gardeners who find that they create differently once in the garden than on paper; this gardener draws up charts only to forget them (or fling them away) in an exuberance of on-site design. Whatever type of gardener you are, you can use the following meditation, which encourages self-awareness and provides a basis for appropriate planning.

Just as a gardener must consider the sunlight and soil of the garden space, so you must consider your personal desires and tastes in planning a garden space—or in continuing the development of a space where you already garden. This meditation assists in that process. Like the earlier part of this winter meditation, you can do this in solitary fashion, writing about or thinking through the questions, or you can examine these questions in meditative conversation with your friends.

Our gardens are archetypal spaces, dreams we create from and with our plant companions. Thus it is important first to consider what spaces occur in your dreams. If you remember and record your dreams, examine them with the following questions in mind. If you do not, try incubating a dream: before sleeping, ask yourself the following questions and let your dreaming mind answer. Finally, if you find it difficult to recall dreams at all, consider these as questions about your preferences. Put yourself in a meditative or trancelike state and "dream up" the answers, or just write the answers as quickly as you can, not editing and changing them but using writing as a means to unfold your dreams.

When you have finished this exploration, make a list of any specific features that have appeared and that could be incorporated into your waking garden. For instance, if you frequently dream of sitting quietly by a lily pond, consider creating a small water garden. Even a large urn filled with water and sporting a metal lotus sculpture will bring your outer life into alignment with your inner one.

Next, search your memory for emotionally important garden images. The following questions will help you locate them:

- Is there a plant or plants that have deep resonance for you because of a connection to a loved one?

- Is there a public or private garden where you have spent especially meaningful times?

- Are there any gardens in art, film, or literature that have a special hold over you?

- Do you recall any myths, fairy tales, or legends in which gardens are important and that have inner significance to you?

You are now about to do some archetypal work—work with images found in dreams, myths, and art—that will assist you in your garden planning. Two lists follow, one of plants that often have symbolic meaning, the other of symbolic objects that might be incorporated into your garden. Examine them carefully, and select any that have deep resonance for you. Do not edit your responses; even if something seems "not spiritual enough," if it calls to your soul, it is something that should be respected.

Plants

acacia	grapevine		
alder	ivy		
apple	lily		
aster	lotus		
berry	oak		
birch	olive		
bluebell	palm		
cedar	pine		
clover	poppy		
daisy	rose		

Objects

bell	flag
bench	frog
bird	horse
boat	lamp/lantern
butterfly	mirror
cauldron	shell
clock	steps
column	stone
door	wall
fish	water

Next, consider the following shapes. Once again, respond immediately, without permitting self-consciousness to intrude. Ask yourself which of these shapes makes you feel most comfortable, and which are most exciting or stimulating. If there are any you have no feeling for, or any that inspire strong negative feeling, note that too. (Be aware that lack of reaction could hide a negative reaction.)

Shapes

circle	straight line
square	curved line
triangle	vertical line
rectangle	horizontal line
oval	diagonal line

Finally, consider the following colors and qualities of colors. Do not consider whether you like or dislike the colors; rather, find associative words for them. For instance, associations to blue might be heaven, depression, the sky, coolness. Don't worry if the associations don't always seem logical. When you have finished these lists, you will decide how to use them, so don't worry whether or not you "like" the colors or the combinations—yet.

Colors

black	orange
blue	pastels
bright colors	red
brown	silver
clear colors	tan
dark colors	violet
gray	white
green	yellow

Now begin combining these lists. What plants and colors combine well with what shapes and objects? Remember that you can divide your garden into various sections that reflect your different aspects. You may, for instance, find that you love blue but also adore roses. As blue roses are still a natural impossibility, you'll have to be imaginative in creating a blue/rose garden. Underplanting crimson roses with blue-faced pansies might appeal to you, or placing roses against a backdrop of tall blue delphinium. Similarly, use your new knowledge of which shapes and objects call to your inner gardener to decide on basic structural features for your garden.

You have now done the preliminary work to begin planning your garden. As you begin designing borders and ordering plants, use this new knowledge in helping to make selections. If you find that birds are an important image of the soul to you, you may wish to plan for bird-friendly plantings or center a part of the garden on a bird sculpture—or both. If you respond to the image of a shady cave, you may want to build some arbors or establish some hedges. What is most important is that the garden represents your creative, dreaming self, rather than that it follow any preset pattern.

You'll find more ideas in the following chapters on ways to integrate the inner and outer garden. Before you begin your planning, journal (talk to yourself) or dialogue (talk to someone else) about how you employ your creative self most effectively. If you have gardened before, ask yourself what gardens you have created that were most effective. What creative process did you use? Did you plan thoroughly on paper, then execute that plan? Did you work on-site, changing and altering things as you felt inspired? Did you work in a solitary fashion? Did you ask others' opinions?

You are a unique gardener; there has never been a gardener exactly like you before. To create the garden that is most perfectly, uniquely your own, you must grow in self-knowledge. Some of that takes place as you learn, in garden planning, how your creativity is most readily expressed. Similarly, you will learn about yourself through the tasks of gardening. Advice from others can be useful, but just as no one can dream for you, no one can create your garden for you either.

Spring:
Consecrating the Garden

Spring is the border between dreams and life.

Full of risk and potential, spring is not always pretty, comfortable, or easy. It is a season of mud and storms, weeds and litter, as much as it is a time of new growth and delicate blossoms. Most importantly, spring grants the gardener a chance to engage the creative mind with the realities of matter. Each spring the gardener meets the garden afresh. Some perennials spread astonishingly. Others have self-seeded tiny sprouts of themselves. Yet others show no green, week after week, until you admit they have been lost to winter's chill. Trees and shrubs suddenly reveal last year's growth. Lawn destruction by grubs is suddenly visible. Weeds you were certain you'd eradicated come back. The garden is not the same garden it was last year. Each spring the garden is a new garden.

Thus spring is the time for consecrating, or reconsecrating, the garden. This is especially true if you are gardening in a new location, but the reconsecration of a familiar garden should be part of your annual cycle. The following ritual is intended for those establishing a new garden, with variations for a new year in an old garden following.

As a gardener, you may have left a garden behind in your last home. If you are sufficiently near your previous garden to return to it, or if you have not yet left for your new garden, find a plant or shrub you especially love. Carefully dig it up and wrap its roots well for transport, for part of building your new garden will be to place something of your old garden within its confines.

If you are no longer near your previous garden but are in a similar gardening zone, find a plant (or seeds for a plant) of a variety you favored there. For instance, if you had a wondrous stand of hollyhock that, in your journaling, you realized you will miss desperately, find a good local supplier of hollyhock and purchase several of the same (or similar) variety.

Don't simply walk into any store and buy the first plant you see. Part of this ritual's intent is to re-root yourself, to make the connections in your new community that will make your garden-self flourish. Thus the research that you do to find the best plant source is a vital part of the ritual. Ask neighbors what nursery or garden center they recommend most highly; make some telephone calls to see which shops seem most informed and cooperative; find a good bookstore with local magazines, and browse the ads in a local or regional gardening publication.

If you have moved to a substantially different gardening zone from your last garden, your ritual will be the same as above but with a slight difference: you will have to decide what plant to make the centerpiece of your ritual. Look to your dreams, memories, and associations for suggestions. Have you dreamed, for example, of a certain kind of tree, bush, or flower? Is there a plant that has significant positive memories for you, perhaps because a beloved grandparent or friend grew it? Is there a plant with which you have positive associations through mythology or art? Once you have settled on a plant with personal meaning for you, seek out a living example of it just as suggested above.

Before you purchase the plant, learn as much as you can of its requirements for sun, soil, and water. Then explore your land to determine the best location for it. Once you have selected that, prepare to consecrate the area by drawing a circle around it, calling down the powers of earth and sky as you do. Create this circle

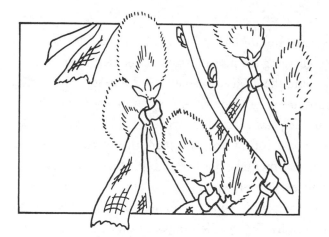

with a garden hose (a good way to make sure that the shape and size is what you want), with flour, or with another temporary marker. Then dig a preliminary hole, visualizing digging through to a new life, one that is even happier and more spiritually fulfilling than your earlier years. Fill the bottom of the hole with compost or a similar soil addition, thinking of the way even the less-happy parts of your earlier life will feed this new life you are growing.

Purchasing your new plant during a waxing moon attunes you to ancient traditions of planting and also reminds you of the monthly cycle at your new home. When you take the plant home with you, keep it indoors overnight, set prominently within your home—on your altar or mantel, in the front hallway, even on the headboard of your bed. Spend at least an hour getting to know the plant, admiring its structure, feeling its leaves or bark, carefully touching its various parts. (If you are planting from seed, open the seed packet and hold the seeds while meditating on their potential and observing them carefully.) Speak to the plant of your hopes and wishes for it and for your new garden.

The next day, tie a dozen or so small strips of cloth to the plant, decking it from root to tip with little streamers. As you tie each strip, speak aloud a prayer for the future of your garden. Such plant petitions are an ancient tradition in both the Celtic lands and in Japan, where white prayer strips flutter in the wind to remind the divinities of worshipers' petitions. In this ritual, you tie yourself to innumerable other seekers who have sought abundance and peace.

Carry the plant ceremoniously to the place you have selected. Complete the preparation by enlarging the prepared hole if necessary to fit the root ball. Carefully lower the plant into the ground, visualizing the newcomer thriving and growing amidst your garden's other plants. Ask for help in setting down roots in your new garden. Position the plant as firmly in the earth as you yourself wish to be planted, then fill the hole with soil. Water your plant thoroughly as you pray for sufficient resources (emotional, mental, physical, and spiritual) to sustain your new life.

For the next week, water the plant daily. At the end of one complete moon cycle, untie the petition-prayers and bury them near the plant. You are now ready to commit yourself to establishing a garden in your new home.

If you are resanctifying a garden for a new year, you may use the same ritual, altering it in one of two ways. You may establish the margin between your dreaming, creative self and your active, actualizing one by planting a tree, shrub, or plant that comes from the winter work above. Making your first seasonal act the ceremonial planting of a new rose bush of which you have dreamed, for instance, can establish the pattern of sacred consciousness you wish to encourage.

Similarly, the exchange of plants with dear friends is a happy spring ritual. Perennials of which you have a surplus can be traded for those overtaking a friend's yard. Such a seasonal ritual can be done with a group, moving from garden to garden and culminating with a spring feast, or it can be done by a pair of friends, lovers, or sisters who use this day to strengthen their bonds of love as well as their garden's bounty. Find ways to share emotionally as you share your plants.

Other reconsecration rituals for the spring garden are:

- Cleaning and sharpening garden tools before the first use. Painting symbols of abundance on their handles makes this an especially meaningful experience.

- Building a fire in a contained fire pit (see chapter 4) to eliminate the winter's windfalls.

- Gifting friends with early flowers tied with ribbons on which wishes for the new season are written.

- Holding a feast on the first sunny spring day.

- Decking the gateways to the garden with sprigs of new growth or early wildflowers.

Even drinking the year's first cup of tea on the patio can be a ritual if it is done consciously, if it's repeated with intent to link the years together, and if it corresponds to your dreaming self's needs.

Summer:
Working the Garden

In summer, the garden wakes from our dream into its own reality.

In winter and spring, we live in our dream garden: lush, perfect, ever-blooming, without a weed or pest in sight. Deer never eat the lettuce there, nor squirrels the juicy strawberries. Neither grass nor gardeners ever get crabby. There is always enough sun, always plenty of rain, in the garden of our dreams.

Then summer comes.

Rain drowns the seedlings, or harsh, early heat bakes them. Pea vines wither without flowering. Squirrels tear apart the bean shoots. Roses grow leggy, with few buds and thick leaves.

And the weeds—the weeds outgrow both the garden plants and our own energies.

Suddenly there are endless tasks, all calling for our attention at the same time. The tomatoes need to be staked, the coleus pinched back. Where is the net cover for the strawberry bed? Where is that article about slug traps?

If winter is dreaming and spring is hope, summer is work. Winter is nouns, like *rose* and *lily*. Spring is adverbs: *possibly, eventually*. Summer is the season of the verb: *hoe, fertilize, mulch, tie, pinch, prune*.

For those who see meditation as holding still—for those who believe the soul is higher than the body—summer is the garden's least spiritual time. It is a time of action, not contemplation. Yet summer is a magical season to those who recognize that meditation is a dance of consciousness through flesh, that prayer is grace in movement, that soul and body are one. The miracle of life unfolds before our eyes daily, even hourly. The challenge is simple: to remember to look.

Of all the seasons, summer is the one that brings the most accessible spiritual lessons, for we garden as we live. The special challenges and joys of gardening tell us much about ourselves, if only we listen. Learning to listen while we move through our life, through our world, is one of the great gifts of the summer garden. Gardening gives us the gift of unified consciousness: mind, soul, and hand working as one. If we learn to be conscious while working our gardens, we can become similarly conscious elsewhere: in the office, on the street, in the bedroom.

The summer rituals and meditations of the gardener are unique, individual, and solitary. There is no formula for them, for they must emerge spontaneously and organically from the gardener's own soul.

Yet how can it be ritual if it is so spontaneous and individual? Is ritual not an act repeated over and over, with intent and with meaning?

Yes, ritual is that. And your spontaneous activities in the garden are indeed ritual, because in each action, you reach through time to connect with all other gardeners who have performed that action. You connect with every gardener who has ever bent from the waist or knelt in that season on that piece of ground. You touch with your spirit every gardener who has ever reached a hand up into a tree to test a ripening fruit, whether that gardener was a millennium ago in the eastern Mediterranean or a year ago down the block.

Gardening is like time travel, like falling through a space warp. Sometimes you sense the others around you, those gardeners of the past—perhaps even of the future—tending, nurturing, yearning toward harvest. A mystical sense of timelessness often falls over gardeners hard at work on a repetitive task. The reverberation of that repeated motion calls forth an echo from all the other gardeners who have swung their arms in just that way, whose legs have felt just that strain, whose eyes have squinted in the same way against the beaming sun.

In the most profound of gardening meditations, you experience moments of complete unity with past and future. Prepare your mind for these moments by acknowledging throughout the gardening year the presence of those who have gardened before you. Find out, if you can, about ancestors who tilled the soil, and incorporate some part of their gardens in your own.

Some ways to do this are:

- Visit an ancestral homestead and bring back a small rock or a flagstone.

- Plant a species or variety from the country of your origin.

- Plant something a deceased relative favored.

- Honor the previous residents of your land by learning all you can about their identities and ways.

- Plant native plants, especially those favored by indigenous peoples of your area.

- Give your garden a name (or name its various sections) that reflects the heritage of the area or of your family. Put the name up on a board hanging above an arbor, on the gate, set into a path, or otherwise incorporated into the garden's structure.

As you become aware of yourself as one gardener in the great river of time, you become conscious of the echoes of other space-times. Your eyes have not been the only ones to linger on a budding rose. Let your consciousness expand to include all those who have seen just such a flower in just such light.

Not only does gardening open temporal doorways linking you with distant others, it also permits you to go more deeply into your own soul to learn lessons that can elude you elsewhere. Every action you take is—in miniature—the drama of your life. If you find yourself having difficulty thinning carrots, ask yourself what other areas of your life have been permitted to grow unchecked because you dread making choices. If you continually forget to mow the lawn, ask yourself what within you wishes to grow weedy and wild. If you plant tomatoes for another but dislike them yourself, consider what other parts of your private space you have given over to that person.

Here are some other points to notice about yourself as a gardener:

- Do you tend to garden at the same time each day or whenever the mood strikes you? How does this reflect your attitude toward other parts of your life?

- Is there a time of the day that draws you to the garden most regularly? What do you do during that time in winter or when the weather is rainy? Do you garden to avoid something less pleasant? If so, why do you keep that unpleasantness in your life?

- Which gardening tasks are most distasteful to you? What life tasks do they recall?

- How do you treat others who come into your garden? Do you prefer to garden alone or to have company? What can you learn about your needs for privacy and company from this?

- When do you find yourself becoming impatient with the garden? What does this impatience remind you of in your nongardening life?

There is no need to set aside special time to probe these questions. Let them become part of your meditative consciousness in the garden. Hold up each garden action to the light of your higher consciousness and examine how it connects to your life, to your character, to your desires and dreams. You will soon find that there is no action you take in your garden that is not a symbol of your inner conflicts and potential.

Fall:
Clearing the Garden

Fall is fullness and emptiness all in one.

There is the fullness of the cupboard filled with jellies and pickles and preserves. There is the fullness of the cellar, with its root crops and cabbages. There is the fullness of memory, of splendid days and rainy ones, of successes and of failures.

But there is emptiness as well. The empty fields and the empty garden beds stretch out. There will be more later—next year, when the yarrow sprouts its ferny greens and the roses throw out stiff new canes and the herbs are sweet in the evening air. But that will be later, next year, not now. Now there is only ending.

The rituals of harvest are therefore rituals both of great feasting joy and of sadness and loss. It is appropriate to celebrate the dead at harvest rituals, as the Celts who gave us Hallowe'en knew. For harvest is a time when we must acknowledge the dreams we have held and lived, knowing that some can never be fulfilled, while others come again in dreams and in gardens yet to be.

Many gardeners neglect to ritualize the loss and sadness of the garden's ending, putting off or avoiding tasks that—if well performed—make the garden and its sleeping plants more comfortable in winter and early spring. Such avoidance is not surprising, for we live in a culture that celebrates youth (springtime) and neglects age (fall). In coming to terms with the fall garden, we must come to terms with our own aging and eventual death. How we feel about them affects how well we perform our fall rituals.

To prepare fully to celebrate the fall garden, first make up a list of the tasks the garden requires. They may include:

- Mulching perennial beds
- Putting in spring bulbs
- Digging out and dividing perennials
- Digging out and storing bulbs
- Pruning
- Raking

- Composting leaves
- Covering roses and other tender perennials

Are there some tasks you avoid? Why? What other life tasks do they recall, and how do you feel about them? Is there any connection between or among the tasks you avoid?

Similarly, consider the tasks that give you pleasure. What do you enjoy about them? Are they sociable or solitary tasks? What other life tasks do they recall, and do you react to those tasks in a similar fashion? Is there a way to extend the enjoyment you feel at some tasks to those you do not enjoy?

Notice your body's sensations as you work in the fall garden. Note how the air's chill affects you. Note how you feel about touching and transporting the dead and dying plants of the garden. Become conscious of the way the plants die. Some die back a bit at a time until finally they stand there, still and gray. Others die suddenly, sometimes without even changing color, just collapsing in a greenish heap. Explore your memories of the deaths of loved ones, including loved pets. Let the plants stand in for those losses. Let yourself grieve the losses, too, of dreams and ambitions, of loves and friendships. Fall is the time of passing, time both to remember and to let go.

Here are some suggestions for small rituals to memorialize your losses:

- Dedicate a section of the garden to a lost loved one. Position a plaque or other memorial within it. In fall, place dried plants and flowers all around the memorial.

- During the year, save up emblems of habits you wish to break or negative thoughts you wish to release. As you burn fall leaves, burn those emblems as well.

- Similarly, you can use fall bonfires to release attachments that are now moribund or dead. You may be tempted to throw a picture of a former lover on the fire, but it's better to throw love letters or emblems of the former relationship so that healing can take place together with the potential of a healthier connection with the former friend in future.

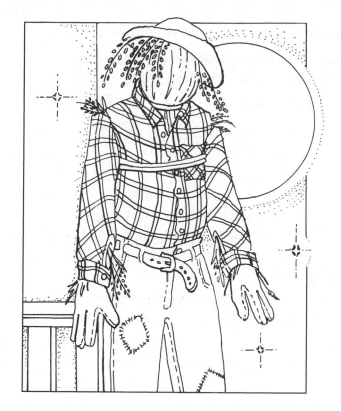

- Tie together long grasses into sheaves and place them on your porch or near the driveway, or stuff some old clothes with straw or leaves and set it near the house. These corn dollies, a European tradition, represent both the harvest and the spirits of the deceased, who rejoin us at that time.

But fall is not only losses. Harvest is a time of fullness and joy as well, as our national festival of Thanksgiving reminds us. Whether you have used your garden for a few bunches of pansies or grown crates of tomatoes, there are harvest rituals that can symbolize the joy and pleasure you have taken in your garden's cycle.

- Examine whether any plants in your garden have special resonance to living individuals. Each fall, give some part of that plant to the person, together with a letter or poem expressing your love and gratitude for their affection or support.

- Set aside some portion of your harvest to share with friends.

- Give some of your harvest, or a monetary contribution representing it, to a soup kitchen or homeless shelter.

- Give of your time: volunteer for an activity that assists your community.

These rituals take on greater meaning if you perform them annually for many years. Ritual forms the backbone of traditional communities. When you ritualize your garden's year, the great events of your life become reflected in your activities. You'll remember a particular harvest festival as the last one a loved one attended or the last before a welcome child was born. You'll remember grinning with the joy of a new job, clinking glasses with a friend about to move to another state, cheering on a child attempting new tasks. And you will remember them within the context of the repeating ritual of the garden year.

Do not leave the establishment of garden rituals to chance. They emerge in any case, for ritual is what humans do, but your individual and unique garden rituals have more force and power if you design them consciously, considering the meaning you wish to express and finding appropriate symbolic gestures that do so.

As your garden grows, so does your gardener's soul. As fall passes into winter, you enter the dreamtime of the garden and begin to create anew the self that makes the garden of your dreams.

Three
Care of the Soil

Erce

Erce, Erce, Erce,

mother of Earth,

hail to thee, Earth,

mother of men.

Be fruitful now;

fill yourself with food

for your children's use.

• • • • • •

Æcerbot, an eleventh-century Old English "Field-Remedy" charm

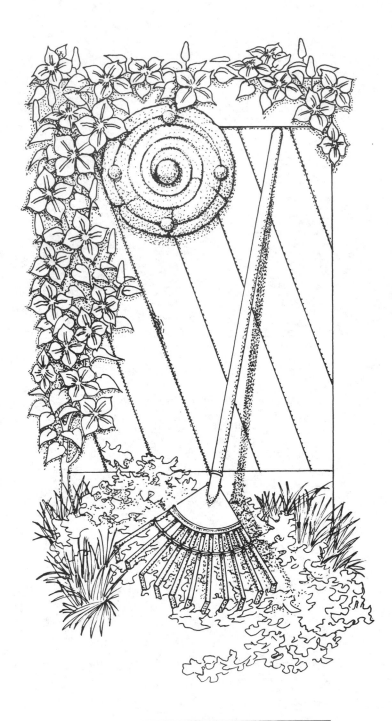

CARE OF THE SOIL

Ancient Egyptians saw the earth as Geb, a squat little man over whom stretched the vast, dark sky goddess Nut, her belly tattooed with rainbows. In Japan, the earth was Ukemochi, from whose fertile body all food sprang: corn from her forehead, rice from her belly, small beans from her nose, large beans from her thighs. The Igbo of Africa called the earth Ala, a goddess in whose shrine harvest festivals were held. The Cherokee honored Selu, Old Corn Mother, who fed her grandchildren with her own body.

"Earth goddesses," such fecund divinities are called, or "earth gods." But the term is slightly inaccurate, for "earth" includes mountains and deserts, oceans and rivers—places where plants do not readily grow. It would be thus more accurate to call such divinities "soil goddesses" and "dirt gods." For it is the soil, nurturing and supporting the plant life we depend on, that these wise cultures honor.

It is easy to understand why subsistence communities honor the soil. Farming people cannot control the weather or the seasons—the gods of those powers were propitiated, not loved—but they can increase their chances of a good harvest through careful land management. This is the case today, just as it was in the past. But in the past, and in traditional societies today, producing food from the earth was part of religious life, one shared by the whole community.

In such societies, techniques for increasing crop yield were conveyed through myth and ritual. The African earth goddess demanded that her followers leave a corner of each field unplowed; this wild patch attracted beneficial animals, insects, and birds. Among the Slavs of eastern Europe and Russia, the goddess Mokosh brought abundance to those who fed her furrows with flour and milk at spring plowing, a ritual that symbolized the need to regularly return nourishment to the soil.

If ancient and tribal cultures saw the soil as having human form, we hint at the same spiritual insight when we speak of rich soil as *humus*—a word having the same etymological root as *human*—for when we care for the soil, we care for ourselves. We care, as well, for our descendants. As the Native American proverb goes, "We did not inherit the earth from our ancestors; we are borrowing it from our children."

Yet it is hard to sustain a worshipful attitude toward the soil today. Contemporary culture—which has given us DDT, flavorless tomatoes, and agribusiness in less than a century—disdains the slow processes of soil building. "It's easy to grow flowers like these," claims a grinning spokesgardener, showing off chemically swollen flowers and impossibly green lawns to viewers whose only potato patch is on the couch.

Easy? Yes, it is. But African mythology warns us of the limitations of focusing on immediate yield without concern for the future.

Sabulana, a Gardening Heroine

Once, they say, a girl named Sabulana lived in a village on the edge of the forest. Food was plentiful in her village. No one ever went hungry, for the village gardens grew huge crops of okra and peanuts, beans and yams. There was wild honey and fruit from the forest for dessert. Life was good for the people of her village.

When Sabulana was a little girl, her people practiced the old ways. They left a corner of the field unplowed in honor of the goddess of the soil. In her honor, they never worked on Thursdays, resting with the earth. They saw all women as images of the goddess. In return, the goddess gave them food.

But as years passed, people stopped practicing the old ways. Some derided them as superstition: why obey those silly old rules? Others were lazy: why follow old rules when life was easier without them? Still others were greedy: why leave those corners unplowed when more crops could be planted there?

Slowly, Sabulana's people forgot the goddess's rules. And slowly, food became less plentiful. One year the bean crop failed. We can live without beans, people said. And so they did. But the next year the peanut crop failed. Then the yams. Each year, food grew more scarce.

The years passed. Farmers still plowed each spring, but barely a sprout came up. Weeds invaded the gardens and grew so fast they towered over even the tallest man. Women put their hands into old tree stumps, trying to find honey, and pulled them out screaming, their hands bleeding from the stings of starving bees.

People began to die. No one could figure out why food was so scarce. Had there not always been food? Their leaders invented magical ceremonies, but none worked. It occurred to none of them to connect the lost old ways with the shortage of food.

People squatted miserably before their houses, moaning for hours at a time. Little children sat and stared, their swollen bellies full of air. People grew so weak that they could not even look for food. Hopelessness set in throughout the village. The few beans left over from planting were devoured. People even ate their leather shoes and capes. They drank dirty water every few hours, hoping the dirt would make the empty feeling in their stomachs go away.

Sabulana felt the pain as much as any of them, but she was not hopeless. Optimistic and determined by nature, she believed that something could be done. "Let me see," she thought. "I was five when the gardens started failing. What was life like before that? Were we doing something differently?"

While everyone else sat and stared at the ground, wishing the hunger would stop, Sabulana pondered. As she considered the problem, she remembered a place in the forest called the grove of the ancestors. No one went there anymore, because they were afraid of ghosts. But the ancestors—they would certainly know how things were done in the old days!

In the old days there had been food in plenty. So Sabulana pulled herself to her feet. Slowly and painfully, supporting herself on a stick she'd fashioned into a crutch, she moved toward the grove.

As she reached it, she felt a chill of fear. She'd heard tales about this grove, how people sometimes disappeared into it. But she would soon be dead anyway, she told herself. And everyone else would be dead with her if she did not find out what the ancestors knew.

The grove, dark with the shade of old trees, was cooler than the plain where the village stood. Sabulana dragged herself over gnarled roots. The cold was unfamiliar to her, whose skin felt the burning sun all day. At the center of the grove she found an open spot. There she sat down, holding her walking stick in front of her like a weapon. There she waited.

Suddenly there was a rush of wind.

She felt the ancestors before she saw them. Slowly they emerged, big headed and long legged. They stood around her like a dark forest. They began to hoot and cackle at her. The noise was deafening.

"Ancestors, I am Sabulana," she called over the din. They waved their bony arms and moved toward her threateningly.

Sabulana was not sure what they could do to her, nor did she know how to defend herself. As they grew closer, screaming at her, she suddenly decided what to do.

She began to sing. They were screaming like babies, so she sang them a lullaby. She sang in a thin, piping voice full of fear and hunger. But she sang bravely, verse after verse.

The ancestors formed a ring around Sabulana. They stared at her and pointed. One began to cry; another sniffled. The girl sang the lullaby all the way to the end. Then there was silence in the grove. Finally, an ancestor woman spoke.

"That lullaby. I sang it to my baby who died when he was an infant."

Another spoke. "It was the song my little sister liked the best, the one who drowned in the lake."

There was silence again. And then the oldest of the ancestors said, "Girl, what do you want?"

Sabulana said, "Ancestors, we are starving. We do not know why. Tell us what you did to raise crops that was different from what we do now."

The ancestors leaned forward. "Only because your song recalls our human life to us," the oldest mother said, "will we tell you. We do not interfere with your lives. We leave you alone and, in return, you remember us with fondness and some fear."

Sabulana bowed to the oldest mother. "But you will help us now? Tell us what to do?"

There was a silence. Then another ancestor spoke. "Do you remember to leave the corners of the fields unplowed?"

Sabulana looked up at her, puzzled. "Why? The extra crops that grow there..." Then she remembered that no crops were growing at all.

A second ancestor spoke. "Do you always rest and worship the goddess of earth on Thursdays?"

Sabulana shook her head. "Thursday is a day like any other."

There was silence. Then the oldest ancestor spoke again. "You transgress against the rules of our mother, the earth. No wonder you are starving. Why should she feed such rude children? You must follow her ways again."

Sabulana nodded. She remembered, just barely, how she used to play in the sun on the Thursday holiday. She remembered people praying over their meals of meat,

thanking the animals who died for their food. And she remembered those bird-filled little corners for weeds where she played hide-and-seek there in the fields. So *that* had been the reason!

"Now," said the oldest elder, "you must go. You are near to dying. If you stay here, you cannot even become a ghost like us, for you have had no children and cannot be an ancestor. Hurry. Get back to your village. Pray with your people."

Sabulana hopped and crawled across the field to the village. She was indeed growing weaker. She pulled herself along, feeling the strength dying in her legs. After falling several times and pulling herself to her feet, she reached the round houses of the village.

"Listen," she began to yell, but a wave of dizziness hit her. She held herself up on her staff. Curious, everyone at their doorsteps looked up at her. But they were too weak to move.

"We have wronged our mother, the earth!" Sabulana said, as loudly as she could manage. "We are starving because she is angry."

Sabulana began to sway with exhaustion and hunger. As people looked on, she fell to the ground. "Is she dead?" a person nearby asked, not really caring, because so many died these days.

But Sabulana did not die. Lying on the ground, she had a vision. Before her she saw the earth goddess, a giant woman with a kindly face, and she saw the ancestors kneeling before the goddess. She could hear them begging for the goddess to forgive the people of her village, to give them another chance. And she saw a smile light the goddess's face as she nodded.

Sabulana fainted. When she came to, someone was holding water to her mouth. She drank, then opened her eyes wide at what she saw.

Everywhere trees hung with fresh fruit. Children pulled berries off low-hanging bushes and stuffed them into their mouths. The gardens were growing so fast she could almost hear the sound of the plants as they pushed up through the soil. Animals were walking up to the hunters, who shot them in amazement.

Sabulana's eyes closed again, this time in happy sleep.

Time, Space, and Dirt

If there is one thing that garden experts agree on, it is the importance of soil improvement and maintenance. There is similar unanimity that composting—the production of rich soil from garden and kitchen waste—is the most efficient way to create better soil. Rich soil, full of the nutrients that plant life depends on, has a friable texture that permits roots to penetrate deeply, producing greater yields for the gardener. Yet the benefits of such soil extend beyond the garden gate. Such soil is stable and less prone to erosion than poorer soils. It is also nature's recycling factory, freeing elements previously bound in organic form to provide nourishment for more growth. Yet the gardener who composts regularly and efficiently is the exception rather than the norm. Even green witches—ecologically minded practitioners of earth religions—may rely on quick-fix fertilizers rather than soil-building and the soul-building that accompanies it.

There are two reasons gardeners offer to explain why composting is not a more integral part of their daily lives: time and space. Composting seems to demand a great deal of both. Articles showing rugged, smiling people turning their three carefully layered compost heaps discourage those whose property seems too small for such an effort, as well as those whose crowded schedules seem to leave little room for complex endeavors.

Yet we make space and time for other activities. We find time to watch a space opera and space for a cat's litter box, time to surf the Internet and space for new shoes. We make time and space for what we value. And we have been taught to avoid, rather than to encourage, processes of decay and decomposition.

Our households are microcosms of our larger society, and soil care is not part of our national agenda—far from it. Thousands of acres of grass clippings are disposed of by being dumped in landfills each summer week in every American city. Our manicured campuses and parks generate huge volumes of green manure that is removed from the lawns it could nurture and turned into waste.

Such consistent avoidance in the face of obvious benefit suggests an underlying mythic or symbolic message that discourages composting. And indeed, our mainstream religious symbols promote a division of humanity from the earth. Its foundational myth describes a god who is neither born as we are born nor dies as we die.

Much has been written about the antisexual subtext of the story of Jesus Christ, born to a woman who conceived "immaculately," without sexual connection to a human man, but few notice the story's anti-soil message. For unlike the body of other resurrecting gods from the eastern Mediterranean, the body of the Christian god is not absorbed into the earth before it is reborn. The body of Jesus never becomes soil—he rises, as the Christian scripture says, "incorruptible." Similarly, his followers are encouraged never to "soil" themselves with sin. Dirt, to the most literal interpreters of this message, must be escaped, cast out, eliminated—certainly not grown and nurtured.

Earthworms in the basement, composting toilets—these evoke shudders of distaste from most people, for we are a culture under the spell of an unsoiled divinity. In this context, soil building is a spiritually radical move. The old rituals of Sabulana's village supported a reverence toward the earth, but the rituals of our daily life indicate a disdain for dirt, for the humus of humanity. We especially resist acknowledging the connection of our own bodies to the process of decay and decomposition. Why is it that the most instantly popular nineteenth-century invention was Thomas Crapper's indoor flush toilet? Because upon the installation of one in the proper Victorian household, there would no longer be a long walk, in full view of neighbors, to the little shack near the hollyhock where one added to the world's supply of waste.

Nowhere is our resistance to accepting our connection with the natural cycle more obvious than in our handling of death. Many authors have claimed that we are a culture that rejects awareness of death. More accurately, our culture refuses to acknowledge decomposition. Christ dies; he does not decay. Similarly, we chemically pickle our deceased so that their loved bodies cannot rejoin the cycle of nature, thus in a perverse way following the example of their resurrected god. Those who wish to decline embalming are offered cremation as the only legal option. Natural decomposition is illegal in many places, or legal only within very narrow parameters, although the "green burial" movement of which many Pagans are part is challenging those laws.

American ambivalence toward decomposition includes an almost fanatic devotion to cleanliness—which is, the aphorism tells us, next to godliness. Commercials ceaselessly urge us to make our laundry brighter and our teeth whiter. And at the same time, news reports show us boats plying the ocean waves looking for somewhere to deposit garbage, cities drowning in debris, and even human "hoarders" crushed by the weight of their litter.

There is a connection. A vast shadow—as that word was employed by psychologist Carl Jung to mean the paradoxical results of repression of natural instincts—is cast by our preoccupation with being "stronger than dirt." In focusing so fiercely on making ourselves and our environment perfectly clean, we have polluted it far more than traditional cultures we deride as dirty.

Thus the first step in creating a truly magical garden is to strive to overcome any residual distaste for the soil we garden in, and to commit oneself to the process of nourishing and replenishing it. As we do so, we can also commit ourselves to self-nourishment. The following meditation can help you focus on the connections between the soil of your garden and the inner resources that nourish your personal gifts.

A Soil-ful Meditation

Before beginning this meditation, take time to cleanse your mind of negative associations with soil and dirt. In your journal or in conversation with a supportive friend, answer the following questions. Take your time; answer the questions in detail. If you are doing this as a solitary effort, this might take several days or even a week to finish; with a friend or a group, allow several hours of intense conversation at least.

- Have I ever criticized anyone else using words relating to soil or dirt? Why? What fears did someone else's behavior regarding dirt give rise to in me?

- When I was a child, did I like to play in dirt? Was I ever criticized for that behavior? Do I remember any specific examples of being criticized for having gotten dirt on my clothing, shoes, or body? Who criticized me? What was my response?

- What emotions do the following words give rise to: soiled, dirty, muddy, unclean, grubby, untidy, slovenly, rotten? Are there any specific incidents or memories these words recall?

- How do I relate to soil and dirt today? Have I ever been criticized or humiliated by having words related to dirt applied to me, my home, my car, or other possessions? How did I react if that happened?

- Am I treating my garden's earth the way I treat myself or the way I treat others? What does this tell me about my own life? Are there ways in which I fail to care for myself, either through active means (such as addictive behavior) or passive ones (such as failing to nurture the self through positive pleasures)? Are there ways in which I avoid taking necessary responsibility for the welfare of others, whether loved ones or strangers? How might I begin to rectify my oversights?

- What happy occasions have I had as an adult that involved soil or dirt? In what circumstances have I given myself permission to take delight in digging or otherwise playing in dirt or mud? What pleasant fantasies can I imagine in which dirt plays a part? What landscapes or paintings in which soil is prominent have pleased me?

After this purification process, you are ready to begin the meditation itself. You need the following:

- A bucket of dirt, preferably from an area where you plan to plant something.
- A small piece of mesh screen.
- A platter or shallow bowl lined with paper or fabric.
- A soil-testing kit (available in gardening centers).
- A small amount of instant concrete (find this at craft stores or building supply centers).
- A knife or other carving implement.
- A pitcher of water.

Gather these implements in an area where you need not worry about clean-up. Outdoors is best, of course, but may be uncomfortable in some seasons and weather. If you perform this meditation inside, you may wish to cover carpets with newspaper.

Friends may join you for this meditation. If they do, encourage them to bring buckets of their own garden soil.

Arrange your meditation space by placing the bucket of soil in front of you, next to the pitcher of water. Arrange the soil-testing kit, mesh, and other implements in a semicircle around the soil.

Begin by invoking the divinities of the soil. In addition to those mentioned earlier in this chapter, you may wish to call on the Greek goddesses Gaia and Demeter, Roman Anna Perenna, Thai Mae Phosop, Polynesian Hainuwele, or Germanic Kornjunfer. Thank the earth divinity (or divinities) for providing all the food you have eaten in your life. Name your favorite fruits, berries, vegetables, and grains, and give individual thanks for each.

Now reach into the bucket of soil and take out a handful. Carefully rub it between your hands. Pay attention to how it feels. Is it dusty or sandy? Does it clump together readily or stick together? Smell it. Does it smell like mushrooms, or is it odorless? Pour it through the mesh screen and examine it further, noticing the number of pebbles and pieces of organic material the soil contains. Are your soil particles fine or heavy? Is there little or much extra material within it?

Next, place several handfuls of soil onto the platter, mounding it toward the center and leaving space between the mound and the edge of the dish. Fill that space with water. Now begin mixing the water and soil into mud; study it as you do. Notice whether the soil becomes slick when the water is added or whether it seems sandy and granular. Imagine that you are a plant drinking from the soil, and imagine how easy or difficult that would be. If you feel so inclined, use some of the soil as paint, and make a design on your face or hands to represent your gardening desires.

Next, use the soil-testing kit to become familiar with how acid, neutral, or base your soil is. Use the same test kit on yourself—your saliva, your tears, even your urine—so that you can compare the soil's composition with that of your own body.

Finally, add some of the instant concrete to your platter of soil. Quickly mix it together and form it into a flat plaque shape—circular, square, or rectangular. Then, using your knife or other carving tool, cut a design into the surface of your plaque. You may wish to use a spiral for life's regenerative capabilities, a circle for life's continuity, a triangle for vitality, or any combination of these. Or you might have another design you favor that represents the abundance you seek.

After finishing the process of familiarizing yourself with your soil, recite the following prayer or words of your own with similar intent:

Gods and goddesses of the soil, thank you for revealing yourself
to me. In return for this knowledge, I pledge to offer you food
when you waken hungry each springtime. And I promise
to give part of each harvest to you in thanksgiving for your
generosity toward your human children. Life comes from you,
feeds on you, returns to you. Let us never again forget you.

After it dries, place the small plaque in your garden as a reminder to yourself to continue the process of soil nurturance throughout the year. Or you may wish to keep it inside, perhaps in the area where you store seed catalogs and other garden-planning tools. Whenever you notice it, stop for a moment to reflect thankfully on the generosity of nature's deities in providing sustenance for their children.

Prayer into Action

Gardening is prayer offered to the earth. It is wordless prayer, prayer of action: kneeling to plant, bending down to weed, putting our hands together to hold ripe fruit. We need no words for the hopeful prayer of springtime when seeds are set, the prayer of our sweat-filled work in summer as we wonder at earth's fertility and the power of growth, or the prayer of gratitude as we harvest the garden's produce.

Like any form of meditation, gardening works on our spirits slowly. Each time we enter the silent garden, we find our minds filled with the roar of worries and plans, but slowly the inner voice quiets as the mind focuses on the tasks at hand. To the passionate gardener, the moment of stillness—when the monkey chatter of daily concerns finally gives way to a deeply sensual attention to the day's light, to the feel of the soil, to the color of the plants—is the truest reason to garden. It is as though earth has become our beloved, and we look and touch and taste her with ecstatic concentration. If this is not prayer, what is?

Yet often we ignore the possibility of prayerful moments in soil nurturance. Raking leaves, carrying out kitchen waste, raking manure into topsoil—these may not call out to us as obviously prayerful moments. Our culturally conditioned aesthetics may blind us to the fact that earth gains more pleasure from being fed a basket of manure than being stripped of a basket of roses. Focus on the task at hand and its beneficial results; after some practice, you will find yourself more open to seeing soil building as a form of worship.

Now that we have examined ways in which the excuse of limited time and space may hide deeper resistances to composting, let us acknowledge that, indeed, today's gardeners often suffer from having too little of those vital commodities. Thus the following ideas for composting assume a busy gardener with limited gardening space. Those interested in establishing a full-scale composting operation will find many books and articles describing the appropriate combination of green and hot ingredients, the schedule for turning to create aeration, and so forth (see bibliography for some of these). The following suggestions for small-scale composting can be used separately or to supplement a larger operation. The compost that results may not be as even in texture, as weed-free, or as richly dark as that made in an often-turned compost pile, but it's better than not composting at all.

Instant Weed Mulch

The simplest way to compost is to use weeds as mulch: just place the uprooted weed on its side in a path or on a mulched bed, where it quickly becomes incorporated into the body of the mulch. This is especially effective early in the season, when the weeds are still small. Larger weeds can also be used as mulch, but the withering bodies will be visible on your paths, while smaller weeds decay so quickly that they're virtually invisible. An important point: once weeds have gone to seed, remove them from the garden. Don't toss that bunch of lambsquarter with its headful of seeds between the rows of tomatoes or you'll live to regret it.

Worm Soup

The kitchen is a great source for compost materials: coffee grounds, vegetable leavings, fruit peels and rinds, and so forth. Even the most frugal consumer creates kitchen waste of the biodegradable sort—dessert for the garden. But don't put leftover animal products in compost, for several reasons: the possibility of infection or infestation, the chance of attracting rodents or other animals, and the slower rate at which animal products decompose as compared to vegetable matter.

If you find it inconvenient to take compostables outdoors daily, there are several ways to store them until you're ready to do so. Several manufacturers can provide specially designed composting pails in which food waste can be stored for approximately a week, or you might use freezer bags, which can be stored in the freezer until you are ready to remove them.

One efficient way to put such compost material into circulation in your garden is through feeding "worm soup" directly to the soil. Run quarts of room-temperature compostables together with a cup of water through a blender, then pour the thin soup either into a compost pit (described below) or directly onto the soil's surface.

If you raise roses, a soup of banana peels makes them especially happy. You don't even need to blenderize the peels. Cutting them up into small strips and digging them into the ground around the roses pleases the bushes just as much. Coffee grounds, too, can be placed directly onto the soil, where they slowly break down. If you are plagued with slugs, ringing sensitive plants with coffee grounds can deter them. Don't drink that much coffee? Ask your local coffeeshop. Some national chains have policies of giving away the grounds to anyone who asks.

Compost Pits

Weeds and leaves decompose when you turn them as instructed by compost masters. They also decompose when you do not. Turning compost speeds up the process by providing air to assist in decomposition. But if you wonder when you'd find time to turn compost, don't let this stop you; it's better to wait two years for the leaves to decompose than to throw them away.

You can create compost by heaping up the leaves and ignoring them. If you have sufficient property, you can designate dump sites you move at regular intervals. Throw leaves and kitchen refuse onto such piles, and you'll enrich the soil effortlessly. You can also use the leaves and other waste to begin the process of establishing a new raised garden bed. Select the location and pile your compost there; then, when you have time, erect the raised bed around the composting material, adding additional topsoil to create good growing conditions.

For those with small gardens, compost pits are an efficient alternative. At the beginning of each gardening season, dig a number of pits, each about one and a half feet wide by two feet deep. Place them around the garden, looking especially for places you wish to plant the following year, for the compost enriches the soil in preparation. You might locate such pits behind screening bushes, but aesthetics don't demand this, as by midsummer the pits will be sufficiently filled so that they won't be noticeable.

As you garden, fill these pits with weeds, thinnings, kitchen waste, and so forth. When a pit is filled, cover it with a bit of topsoil and let it rest. By the next spring, an indentation shows you that decomposition has shrunk the green mass. Planting can occur then, or you can wait another year until the material has been completely absorbed into the soil.

The Three-Pile Process

If you have an area approximately ten feet by three feet to devote to composting, you have the makings of an efficient system. Divide the space into three bins, using wire mesh or similar permanent material. Then, fill one until it is full, tramping or pushing down on the contents so that it's relatively well packed. Move onto the second, then the third. In an average-sized yard, you should have dark, rich compost in bin number one by the time you're ready to empty it and refill it—about eighteen months. If it's not quite ready, remove the almost-cooked compost and dig it into the soil, where it finishes the process. Remember not to include grass clippings or animal products in such a compost pile. Grass clippings decompose too quickly for this slow process, and animal waste may attract unwanted rodents.

Fast-But-Not-Instant Mulch

Some yard waste can be transformed into mulch, which breaks down slowly to enrich the soil, through shredding. Dry autumn leaves are especially adaptable to such treatment. A hand-cranked or electric shredder quickly reduces those bags of yard waste to dusty mulch. Similarly, fallen or thinned branches can be chipped into material for paths and patios, as well as made into a weed-discouraging mulch for vegetable and flower beds. Because such equipment is not needed constantly, you might purchase or rent it with friends. Such mulch is an early form of compost, which needs to be replaced as it breaks down into the soil.

Lawn Clippings

If you have a lawn, you have clippings. If you put the clippings in a pile, you have an odor. But if you leave the clippings on the grass, you have instant lawn food. Here are your choices: mow frequently enough that you can leave the clippings in place; pile them up and turn the compost heap often; or pack them into bags, place them by the curb, and forget the way they create landfill problems. If you want to be a responsible steward of the land, and you don't like turning compost, your choice is clear. Mow weekly (or even more often) in the early part of the season, because this is the time when grass is growing fast, intending to go to seed by midsummer. Once the grass has given up the idea of creating seed heads, it'll relax and so can you. Late summer and early fall lawns require much less frequent mowing.

You can also employ grass clippings as mulch on vegetables and flowers, provided that you use them immediately. Don't leave them for several hours to dissolve into a slimy pile. Spread the clippings in a thin layer wherever mulch is needed. Thin as they are, the clippings dissolve into the soil within a matter of days.

A Simple Prayer to the Earth

The garden will be enriched if you merely dump compost on it, for the nutrients in decaying plants feed the still-living residents of the garden. But composting is a matter of nourishing our own connections with the earth as well as nourishing the earth itself. Taking a moment to meditate on the process you are participating in enriches your soul as well as your soil.

Following the lead of the Slavs and other peoples, you can create a ritual of the first planting each year in which you ceremoniously incorporate compost into the

garden soil while praying for the year's harvest—whether vegetables, fruits, or flowers—to be a good one. Make a conscious and prayerful first addition of compost or other enriching materials to the soil in the spring. Gather together symbols of what you wish to enrich within your life: some paint or ink if you wish to increase your creative output, or some thread if you wish to encourage connection with others, for instance. Make sure these gifts to the earth are biodegradable—nothing plastic!

Fill a pretty vessel—a ceramic pot or a finely woven basket—with some compost or manure, then add your other gifts. Take this vessel to the garden and offer it to the four directions as you invoke the power of the soil. Then, using a shovel or spade as your magical instrument, open the earth to receive your gift and your prayers. Overturn the vessel into the opening in the soil and work the contents together with your garden soil, asking the universe's blessing on your enterprises. When you have completed working this small space, continue incorporating compost throughout the remainder of the garden.

If you use some of the shortcut methods described above, composting is an ongoing process in your garden. If that is the case, take a moment whenever you add fertile substances to your garden—whether it be grass cuttings left behind when you mow, banana soup poured on the roses, or weeds dumped into a compost pit. Give your thanks and state your petition to the earth in words like these:

Earth, you gave this to us once. We have used
it with gratitude. Now we give it back to you.
May it nourish you as you continue to nourish us.

Composting in this way is an ongoing process of making conscious our relationship to the soil as nurturer and upholder of our life. In the rich humus of the garden, more is grown than vegetables and flowers. We also grow our souls—learning to respect and embrace the cycle of life, learning the intricacy of our mutual dependence on the earth, learning to give back rather than simply to take. No more important crop can be grown in the magical garden.

Four
A Course in Marigolds

Harvest Chant

Whose seeds are we? To whom do we belong?

Mother of thunder, mother of trees,

mother of the world, we ask you:

Where did we begin? Where are we going?

Mother of the world, mother of the shaman's pole,

mother of temples, mother of the sky:

Where do we find you? When are you with us?

Mother of our dances, mother of the sun,

mother of fire, mother of all food:

Are you not the only mother we know?

• • • • • •

Kágaba people of Colombia, South America

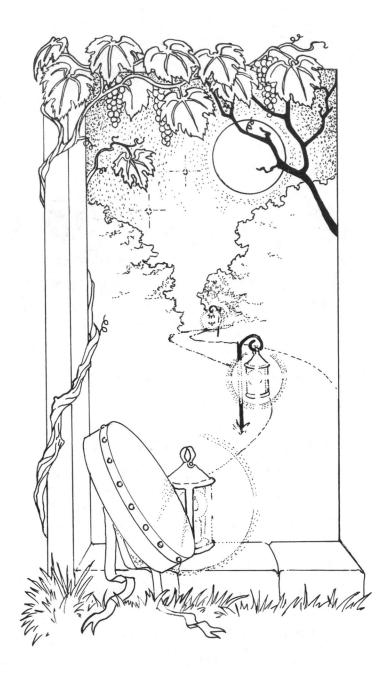

Once upon a time, there were no gardens anywhere in the world. People lived on what fruit they could gather from the surrounding jungles and on what meat they could hunt down in the mountains.

Among these people there was a diligent hunter named Ameta. One day he caught sight of a wild pig, a huge animal with enough meat for many people and for many days. He set off in hot pursuit.

With his dog, Ameta ran and ran, hoping to tire out his prey. But the pig was stronger than any he'd ever seen. It ran on and on and on, deeper into the dark forest.

Ameta and his dog kept pace but could not run the pig to ground. At last they drove it into a clearing. There, in the center under the great trees, a small, dark pool gleamed. The hunter saw the pig rush into the green water, saw the ripples from its passage, saw its tusks sink beneath the mirrored surface.

The pool seemed to be deep, because the pig sank out of sight. In a few days, the hunter knew, the body would rise to the water's surface and would be easy to snare with a net. But by then it might be too decayed to use for food. So Ameta pulled out his knife, cut down a large tree limb, and began to carve a grappling hook.

When the hook was done and connected to some vines, Ameta reached with it into the part of the pool where he'd seen the pig disappear. Again and again he reached, as night gathered around him. His dog snuffled a little at the encroaching darkness, but the determined hunter would not stop.

At last he felt his hook tear into something. Tugging on the vines, Ameta slowly pulled in his prize. As he did so, he imagined the feast they would have that evening when the fine pig was roasted and divided among his kin and the rest of the village.

But what came out of the pool was not a pig. It was a round, hairy ball about the size of a human head. A pig's tusk was stuck through it.

Ameta had a tusk but no pig. The hunter could not understand how the huge pig could have disappeared completely in the small, dark pool. But night was almost upon him, and so he left the forest, taking his peculiar prize.

Back in the village, Ameta examined the ball carefully. It was like nothing he had ever seen before. Milky fluid seeped from the wound when he withdrew the tusk. The object was like an egg or a huge seed.

Not knowing what else to do with his strange prize, Ameta took it out to his father's field the next day. There he buried it deeply in a vacant corner of the field. When his task was done, Ameta mounded the soil atop the object firmly. Then he walked away and forgot all about it.

Only six days later, Ameta heard his father cry out in fright and surprise from the field.

Running to the field where his father stood, hands stretched out, eyes wide, Ameta did not think of the strange seed-fruit he had buried. He did not think of it when he stood by his father's side looking at a ropelike tree twisting its way out of the earth. He did not think of it as the tree tossed a leafy crown into the air and flowered, all within moments of erupting from the earth.

But when the flowers swelled instantly into round fruits, which ripened and dropped to the earth with hard popping sounds, Ameta suddenly recognized the prize from the forest pool. But this time he was not so baffled by the hairy balls falling from the world's first palm tree. Grasping one from the ground, he pulled out his knife and split it in two.

Milk poured over his hands, white juice that felt sticky and tasted sweet when he sucked his fingers. The flesh inside was firm and white, like good pig's meat. Ameta, following the tradition of the hunters of his village, carried the first piece to his mother. She looked at it curiously—she had never seen meat so white as this—but, tasting it, she found it good.

Ameta served the rest of the village from the fruit of his prize tree. The magical pig, he realized, had provided a new kind of meat for his village, one that would serve when the animals had retreated into the hills and forests, one that could be pounded and made into soup and dried and stored against sharp hunger.

· · · · · ·

There are many such tales that would end here, with the miraculous food being brought to the people. But the story of Ameta and his tree goes on to even more mysterious happenings. For this is not only a story about how an important food was given to the island folk but a story as well of the ritual they needed to learn in order to give thanks for the food—and of the woman who came to teach it to them.

The coconut palms flourished on the island. Although none grew so quickly as what Ameta had first planted, soon there was a thick grove of them surrounding the village. Food had never been so plentiful. The children of the village played happily, never knowing the pinch of hunger.

Ameta did not stop hunting, but he often took time to sit beneath the miraculous tree. He made himself a mat of fronds from the tree, and there he would sit and contemplate the greatness of earth's bounty. One day, as he sat thoughtfully, a ripe coconut fell from the tree, straight down onto one of his hands. He leaped aside, but not soon enough. The hard falling fruit tore a long gash down the back of the man's hand.

Blood ran from Ameta and fell onto the palm mat beneath him. As the hunter sucked the cut and complained loudly, villagers ran forth to see the source of the commotion. By the time they reached Ameta, there was more than just a wounded man to gape at.

Beneath Ameta's feet the palm mat was bulging and swelling. It was as though it had come into pulsing life once again. Ameta leaped from it and watched, mouth agape, as the palm fronds curled over upon themselves and formed the shape of a baby.

The baby seemed to be sleeping. Ameta leaned forward and touched the tiny figure with one careful finger. It wriggled a little, then opened its eyes.

Tiny, perfect dark eyes looked out at the hunter.

The little girl drew a long, deep breath and looked up at Ameta. Then she lifted her arms toward him and whimpered.

Without an instant's thought, the hunter picked her up and cuddled her. The girl curled into his shoulder and went peacefully back to sleep.

Behind him, the villagers let out sharp disbelieving breaths. A baby from a piece of dead palm leaves? How could this be? They murmured among themselves as the hunter carried his baby home.

But more miracles were to come. For the next morning Ameta awoke not to the chirping sound of an infant but to happy singing. He rose immediately to shoo away the children who were bothering his baby. But in place of the baby, he found a healthy young girl child who looked up at him with perfect trust and smiled.

"Hainuwele," she said happily, pointing at herself. She had given herself a name.

Hainuwele grew with astonishing rapidity. That second morning she seemed to be about two years old. The next morning she was four. Several days later, her breasts began to bud and, overnight, filled out. Her hips developed curves that same day, and her face lost the roundness of childhood.

The women of the village moved Hainuwele into a solitary hut in order to prepare her for womanhood's blood mysteries. Her mind matured as quickly as her body. Hainuwele seemed to know the village's language at birth. Similarly, she knew all the history and religious traditions without being told. By the time of her welcoming-to-womanhood ritual, one day after she disappeared into the hut, she knew as much as a girl who had prepared for a year.

When she emerged, only a week after her miraculous birth, Hainuwele was a magnificent young woman. The next day, the smallest wrinkles appeared by her eyes.

She called Ameta to her. With some anxiety—for he did not know how to speak to this lovely young woman who, only days ago, had been playing on the straw floor of his house—Ameta went to her.

"I must prepare to die," she said simply. Ameta nodded, for it was clear that she would continue to age as quickly as she had matured. "But I wish to give you something." She instructed him to gather the entire village in the open space beyond the palm grove. He was to do this the next night, when the moon rose full in the dark sky.

Ameta went from house to house, bearing Hainuwele's instructions. Not a single person declined the invitation. They had all been stunned and fascinated by the coming of this miraculous creature into their midst. Although they had not known her long enough to love her, the villagers felt a curious, strong pull toward her that was more than mere curiosity. For each of them, she seemed to recall some forgotten part of themselves.

The next evening, as the moon rose, the villagers gathered as they had been instructed. Even the little ones were there, carried sleeping in the arms of their wakeful parents. The people stood in little groups and couples around the clearing.

There was a sudden stir. Hainuwele appeared, naked except for a garland of flowers around her neck. Even from a distance, it was clear that she had begun to enter middle age. Another day and she would be a crone, and another day after that, she would be a wizened elder. One more day, and death would welcome her.

Hainuwele walked confidently to the center of the clearing. She raised her arms above her head. *Boom!*

The sudden crash startled everyone. As one, the villagers turned to see one of their oldest women standing over a tree trunk on which kava cloth had been tightly stretched. *Boom!* They had never heard a drum before, but the people responded with every fiber of their beings. *Boom!*

Hainuwele began to dance. There had never been dancing in the world before, and so the people stared at her, hypnotized by her whirling hips and darting feet. Then, slowly, they began to move as well. Even those holding children danced. Slowly at first, then with more and more frenzy, the people danced.

Boom! Boom! The drum sang. The people began to shout and sing, songs that would later become parts of their religious ritual but were, that moonlit night, only the sounds of their souls finding song for the first time. *Boom!*

Hainuwele, at the center of the clearing, began to sink into the ground.

No one noticed. They were dancing, they were singing, they were swaying to the drum. *Boom!*

She sank farther. Her feet and legs were completely encased in earth. *Boom!* The earth reached her breasts. *Boom!* Only her head was above ground.

Then she was gone.

But no one noticed. They danced, they sang, they swayed to the drum. All night they danced, until they each, one by one, fell asleep on the dancing ground.

When they awakened, it was dawn. In the center of what had been the clearing there was a jungle of new growth. There were huge glowing fruits, lavish leaves, berries—but none that the people had ever seen before. Slowly, timidly, they approached the entwined plants. A child reached out and took a berry, put it into her mouth, and smiled. Soon everyone was reaching out and tasting and devouring.

Hainuwele was nowhere to be seen. She was gone, gone beneath the earth—or, we should say, her human body was gone. But she remained forever as all the fruits and vegetables that the people would ever need—food that grew from their miraculous visitor and that was tended with her rituals and songs.

Garden Parties and Public Rituals

This myth, from the South Pacific island of Ceram, is one of many legends that emphasize the connection of gardens and rituals. The famous mysteries of Eleusis in Greece—so secret they were never divulged, although perhaps a million people were initiated over a millennium of celebration—seem to have centered on the miraculous transformation of soil and water into living beings. The Iroquois Green Corn dance, the (literally) heart-stopping Aztec sacrifices, the Russian village dances, even the Irish faction fighting at harvest festivals that descended from old rituals of warfare between light and darkness—these were public recognitions that the cycle of the planting year is vital to the maintenance of human life and society.

We have already examined the ways in which the rituals of working the garden provide a framework and a metaphoric context for personal self-analysis and growth. Now we move beyond the individual to examine the ways in which gardens provide both context and metaphor for social connection and celebration as well, for the garden is not merely a place for solitary reverie and insight, although it certainly is that. It is also a place that provides location and materials for celebrations.

These celebrations fall into two categories. Whether Christian or Muslim, Wiccan or Druid or Jewish, individuals and communities mark the cycle of the year in seasonal rituals. They also celebrate personal changes or transitions in ceremonies called rites of passage. People around the world ritualize the year's darkest day: Christians mark it as the birth of their savior, ancient Romans celebrated it wildly as Saturnalia, Jews call it the Festival of Lights or Chanukah, Wiccans gather for winter solstice rituals. Similarly, each tradition finds ways to mark birth, death, and other important life passages. Whether as a wedding under a chuppah or as a handfasting, some form of couple joining is found everywhere, just as every human group has found a way to mourn someone's death while celebrating life.

Sometimes gardens provide the setting for such ceremonies, as when a couple is wed in a public rose garden or handfasted in their own back yard. Gardens also provide materials for celebrations. Holly is cut at winter solstice, daisies form crowns for the Queens of the May, fallen leaves are formed into a harvest centerpiece. Here we explore the connections of gardens and holidays, exploring how best to stage outdoor ceremonies as well as ways to use the garden's products for indoor rituals.

Ritual and Ceremony in the Garden

It is June, and across the nation brides decked in sparkling white veils march solemnly down aisles of lawn to meet their smiling bridegrooms under rented awnings and canopies.

Or it's midwinter, and plywood crèches illuminated with little flashing bulbs suddenly bloom on suburban lawns.

Or it's spring, and children race screaming around the greening yard, looking for brightly colored and carefully hidden hard-boiled eggs.

The neighbors look on from discreet windows or observe as they pass on daily errands and chores. No matter what their religion, they smile acceptingly. Perhaps they feel a twinge of regret at some personal loss or lack; perhaps they resent the neighbors' happiness and luck; perhaps they are irritated at not being invited. But they do not generally feel uncomfortable with these events, despite their basis in a religion not practiced by all citizens.

Yet change that scenario. Let the festival be a late summer bonfire, celebrated by a circle of robed individuals who chant quietly and sway to their own music. Or perhaps it is a dark woman dressed in vivid kente cloth, keening in a African tongue while she sways around the lawn. Or maybe it is a singing spiral of dancers who laugh and nod to each other as they wind in and out upon the velvet green lawn.

Those neighbors who in our earlier scenarios were vicariously enjoying the ceremony or who regretted being excluded from it might have a different reaction to these demonstrations of spiritual belief. Telephone calls to police, suspicious looks in the alley, social ostracism, or active harassment are possible. Those who practice earth-based, tribal, or ethnic religious traditions can face significant prejudice from those who do not understand or who fear their beliefs. Just as the sole Jew in a Christian neighborhood might hesitate to display a menorah at midwinter, those who practice earth-based and goddess religions often fear social, professional, or other ostracism. The maxim that "a man's home is his castle" does not preserve us from gossip and misunderstanding among our neighbors.

Thus, before determining how you might use your yard, patio, or lawn for celebrations of the seasons and of life's passages, you must first analyze how intense is your desire for privacy in your dwelling place. The land-use patterns of one who feels no need to keep beliefs private differs substantially from those of someone who wishes to remain private.

Privacy is not the same as secrecy. You might wear a pentacle to the grocery store, proudly acknowledge your Pagan beliefs at work, and send notes to the children's teachers whenever your religion has been slighted or insulted, but still wish to keep the actual practice of those beliefs private from strangers' eyes. Or you may feel that the practice is enriched by the witnessing of others, whether they believe as you do or not. Do not begin your landscaping plan before you determine how you feel on this vital issue.

To make such a determination, examine your actions in other areas of your life. Would you rather:

- Sit on the front porch or sit in the back yard?

- Seek out popular beaches or seek out private beaches?

- Attend open-air concerts or enjoy music at home?

- See a parade or see a rare wild bird?

- Take a cruise or take a hike?

- Sit in the sun or sit under an arbor?

- Give a speech or listen to a speech?

Those who choose more of the activities in the former enjoy being in others' vision; those who choose more in the latter feel better when shielded from such visual connection. If you are one of the former, you may wish to landscape your property in such a way as to provide ample open space for ceremonies, for the watchful eyes of neighbors may make your event more exciting. However, if you found most of your answers were from the second part of the questions, privacy should be a primary consideration in landscaping. The whole question can be avoided by just staying indoors. But even the most private individual sometimes wishes to feel the moon's light on a crisp winter night or to sniff the scented breezes of late summer while worshiping or celebrating. Careful use of green screens and other devices make it possible to hold some events outdoors.

Even if you are, at this point, quite comfortable with public displays of your belief, consider how permanent you hope to be in your current home. If you plan to live there only temporarily, you probably do not need to be particularly careful about privacy. In addition, many privacy screens take more than one season to attain sufficient height and width for effectiveness. However, if you plan to live in a home indefinitely, you may wish to consider the long-range effects of easily visible back yard ceremonials on your life and those of your housemates, partners, or children. Consider, too, if your need for privacy changes in later years, whether you have ensured sufficient protection for your beliefs.

If you determine that you need little privacy and are comfortable celebrating without concern for prying eyes, you need only consider what landscaping features will make your rituals most enjoyable. Primary among these is a level "floor" for the ritual area. Most urban and suburban lawns look level to the casual eye but quickly reveal small toe-catching unevenness the moment the dancing starts. While it is certainly possible to correct this by bulldozing the entire space and resodding it, that is not exactly a Gaian approach.

Rather, determine what portion of your property will be used for celebration. Assume at least fifty square feet of open area for each participant if you are a jovial and energetic group given to leaping and frisking, or twenty-five square feet per person for more sedentary groups. Thus a group of ten would require an area between 250 and 500 square feet, perhaps a square of fifteen by fifteen or twenty by twenty. Once you have determined the placement of this ritual area, carefully examine the lawn underfoot. A slight slope will not hinder your use, but a drastic one will require an investment in topsoil to bring it up to near-level. If there are only occasional irregularities in the floor, determine whether these are actual holes in the soil or are caused by clumping of the lawn's grass. If the former, simply clear, fill, and reseed. If the latter, you may wish to consider clearing the offending sections and reseeding, especially if yours is a dancing community.

Next, think about your climate and determine which seasonal rituals you are most likely to celebrate out of doors. Even the most committed outdoor ritualist can unflinchingly choose a well-lit and dry living room over a lovely lawn under heavy rain. Deterrents to memorable outdoor rituals include heavy humidity, poor air quality (smog or related trapped pollutants), insect plagues, constant or heavy precipitation, and extremes of heat or cold. If your region is subject to any of these, consider planning your outdoor space for the gentler seasons. Then explore adding any or all of the following seasonal features to your property.

The Garden's Year

Spring Festivals: Equinox and May Day

The cycle of the garden's year begins as its plants begin to wake from their winter sleep.

Weeds are among the first plants to emerge—but those wild plants can be especially healthful to those who have spent winter months without fresh local greens. Dandelions and nettles are among those early arriving weeds, and both are treasured in traditional societies where herbalists know their nutritional and healing value. Wildcrafting early herbs for use fresh in cooking or dried as tea makes a nice personal ritual for this time of year. What you gather depends on your region, so establishing this tradition helps you get more closely in touch with the land around you.

Each season has two holidays. The first is the solar holiday, marking important stages in the earth's journey around the sun. The solstices and equinoxes can vary slightly from year to year, thus although spring equinox—when day and night are equal—is typically March 21, sometimes the sun's movement means that it is March 20 or 22. The same is true of the solstices (summer, the longest day; winter, the shortest day), which occur on June 21 (summer in the Northern Hemisphere, winter in the Southern) and December 21 (the opposite). In some years, the actual moment of the sun's holding still, which is what the German term *sol-stice* ("sun sits still") means, may vary, but most calendars mark these dates as the solar holidays. You may decide for yourself whether it's important to celebrate according to the traditional time or whether astronomical accuracy is more important to you.

The other holidays, called the cross-quarter days, occur midway between the solstices and equinoxes. These descend from the calendrical reckoning of the ancient Celts and are called Bealtinne (Beltane, May 1), Lughnasa (Lammas, August 1), Samhain (Hallowe'en, November 1), and Imbolc (Candlemas, February 1). These holidays have been widely adopted by Neopagans and Wiccans, even those without Celtic heritage. They represent the strength of the season, whereas the solstices and equinoxes represent the turning points.

The vernal equinox is celebrated in many religious traditions that arose in the Northern Hemisphere. This is the season of Christian Easter (a name derived from the Germanic spring goddess Ostara) and Jewish Passover. This seasonal holiday is especially strong for gardeners, who reenter their garden spaces after a winter of planning and dreaming. Springtime celebrations, of whatever religious tradition, celebrate the renewal of vegetative growth and the renewed human hope that goes with it.

If you live in an area where March is usually snowless and mudless, you can mark the vernal equinox by holding an old-fashioned egg hunt. This is a common ritual for Christian believers, but it has pre-Christian roots. In eastern European cultures, the egg symbolizes the sun returning to warm the needy people after a long winter's absence. Searching for eggs was appropriate when people also waited for the sun's gradual return to warm the earth.

To establish a fit setting for an annual egg hunt, look to spring-blooming perennials. Because hiding eggs in flat lawn is a bit boring for searchers, edge your lawn with shrubs that leaf out quickly in the spring as well as lavish numbers of spring-flowering bulbs. Daffodils, which naturalize and spread quickly, offer thick, grassy foliage in which eggs can easily be hidden; spirea's quick leafing offers similar hiding places. You might consider keying the egg's color to that of the blooms; finding a brilliant scarlet egg at the base of a similarly colored tulip will thrill children of any age.

Six weeks later comes one of the most famous springtime celebrations. Like the egg hunt, the maypole—the primary ritual feature of the Celtic feast of Beltane on May 1—is familiar even to those who do not practice European nature religions. However, while the symbolic egg was absorbed into the Christian spring festival, the maypole was less easy to assimilate. The randy rabbit was tamed into the cuddly bunny, but the maypole's obvious phallic meaning could not be so diminished or hidden. Thus the original meaning of the maypole remains, but its celebration is likely to seem quaintly antiquarian to the uninitiated and so could be performed outdoors without undue concern by neighbors.

Maypoles can be permanent or temporary. For the former, you need a sufficiently straight, tall tree—a chestnut, for instance, or an old pine—with no branches lower than approximately eight feet and with lawn surrounding it. If you have such a tree on your property, count yourself lucky, for trees of sufficient size do not grow quickly. A fast-growing tree such as a poplar often does not have a suf-

ficient branchless trunk for the ribbons. However, planting and tending a maypole tree can be a fine investment in your ritual future.

Erecting a temporary "tree" in the form of a tall pole is a viable alternative. You need a pole at least fifteen feet tall; you may wish to attach permanent hooks or Velcro strips near the top on which to mount the ribbons. And you need a means of erecting the pole. A stone-lined fire pit, which can be used for fire festivals as well, makes an excellent location for the pole erection. Dig the pit three feet deeper than you need for the fire, then fill that extra depth with small pebbles. Over the pebbles place large, flat stones, placing one in the center that is approximately six inches in diameter larger than your maypole. When May Day arrives, remove that stone and twist the maypole down through the pebble layer. Short lengths of rope tied to the pole can be used to steady it upright, or tent pegs can hold the ropes, but be careful not to drag them out into the dancing lawn as you place them. Maypole dancers may enjoy tripping across the lawn—but not over rope supports.

To further enhance the setting, consider planting a circle of spring-blooming shrubs at a distance of ten to twelve feet from the pole—rhododendrons, azaleas, and the like if you do not need privacy; lilacs, mock orange, honeysuckle, and other more full-spreading shrubs if you do. Be careful to leave a sufficient opening in the circle—preferably facing east, the direction of springtime—to permit the dancers to enter easily.

An English tradition connected with May Day is morris dancing, with groups of dancers bearing sticks and costumed in matching (often white) attire. England remains the homeland of the art form, with four teams (Abington, Brampton, Headington Quarry, and Chipping Campden) claiming an unbroken historical heritage. Morris dancers are organized in local clubs, which often stage a performance on May Day if requested. In many towns, the local morris dancers greet the sun or otherwise welcome the season in a public performance. Their presence at weddings is also considered good luck, and morris dancers are often eager to perform at handfastings and to lead congregants in a group dance.

A Germanic tradition for this holiday, called Walpurgisnacht, is the preparation of May wine, a combination of a light white wine with sweet woodruff. If you live in a gardening zone where grapes thrive, consider growing enough to make a small amount of May wine (*maiwein*), which is typically a sweet white wine like a Riesling. Sparkling wine is sometimes used and can be delightful. The herb itself is somewhat difficult to find, either as a plant or dried, but you don't need much. In fact, more than a teaspoon of *Galium odoratum* per bottle could be toxic to some people. The heavy, sensuous fragrance of the plant—called in German *Waldmeister*, "master of the woods"—comes from a compound (coumarin) shared with sweet clover and cinnamon. While the fragrance is sweet, the taste is surprisingly bitter, so use a light hand in making May wine.

If you wish to grow it, a small patch of this perennial suffices for many years, or buy a small amount at a reputable herb store or online provider. Then infuse the wine with the herb by placing some sprigs into the bottle and letting it steep overnight or for a few days, and drink to court the energies of the festival. In some Germanic communities in America you can find premade May wine during this season, which is made from a chemical substitute due to regulation of sweet woodruff.

Summer Festivals: Solstice and Lughnasa

Next in the garden's year comes summer solstice, June 21, the year's longest day, celebrated in Christian lands as St. John's Day (sometimes celebrated on June 24), a time for processions through the fertile fields to sanctify them. It is also known in folklore and, following those traditions, in Shakespeare as Midsummer's Night, although in our calendar the solstice is celebrated on the first night of the summer season. Some call this festival Litha, after an old English word for the solstice.

In much of rural Europe, this feast was celebrated with variations of the Catherine wheel—a rotating, blazing wheel representing the sun. Such wheels were rolled down hillsides to be extinguished in cold lakes in Finland; in Cheddar, England, huge wheels of yellow cheese are still rolled around the landscape. Such traditions recall to observers' minds the fact that the sun is ever advancing through the seasons, its huge yellow ball turning the year's cycle over and over again.

Unless your property boasts a convenient hillside leading to a mirror lake, you may find such festivals hard to reenact, to say nothing of being potentially dangerous. However, you can use fire, the primary solstice symbol, in your garden by building and using a fire circle or fire pit, also useful for rituals at other festivals. Such fiery areas can be built in not much more than an hour. Be sure to check local ordinances about open blazes before you host your first event, however. Nothing dampens the spirits like a shrieking fire siren or a citation from the fire marshal.

To create a simple fire pit, locate an area with no nearby flammables—and look overhead! You might not bump your head on a branch ten feet above you, but a tree with branches that low could suffer fire damage. Once you have sited your fire pit, excavate the soil down to the depth you need and the width you prefer. A small fire pit need only be twenty-four to thirty inches in diameter and eighteen inches deep; a large one, big enough for a fire that will glow for hours, could be as big as thirty-six inches across and twenty inches deep. Much larger than that, though, your fires could assume dangerous proportions.

Line your fire pit with stone or brick. A brick fire pit can be most attractive but requires somewhat more work, for you need to excavate more deeply than your desired depth, then add sand as a base for the bricks. A much easier fire pit requires only flagstones for the interior and a collection of interesting boulders for the rim.

Be certain to find flagstones that are small enough to curve nicely around the cauldronlike bottom of the pit. Make certain, too, that you fit the stones tightly for stability and longevity of the structure.

An even simpler way to create a designated bonfire area is to build a fire circle. This requires somewhat more room, because the fire will spread out horizontally rather than being built up vertically. Site as above, being sure to avoid overhanging branches, then outline the circle with pavers or rocks. You can choose to put benches or other seating around the fire, or leave the area around it open. If you use a fire for ritual, be aware that you need to tend it until it is thoroughly extinguished. Following a ritual with a cookout or barbecue is a festive way to use this garden feature.

Building the fire circle or fire pit can be an enjoyable project to share with friends. Once it is in place, celebrate the solstice by plaiting a wheel—of straw, raffia, even newspaper—somewhat smaller than your fire pit's circumference. Twist the material into two long strips and connect them at the center using burnable ties (additional straw, yarn, or twine) to form a cross. Between the arms of the cross, tie additional strips to form a wheel. Then insert four shish kebab or barbecue skewers, evenly spaced, around the outside of the wheel, leaving them extended far enough to rest upon the rim of the fire pit. Build a fire and, once it's blazing, rest the wheel on the fire and watch it burst into flame. As it burns, reflect on habits of thought and action you wish to burn away, and imagine them being purified from your spirit through the solstice fire. Or simply toss the straw wheel onto the fire, again burning away needless habits.

Summer solstice, when the daylight is longest, is one of the primary solar holidays. The calendula, or pot marigold (*Calendula officinalis*), that sun-faced flower, symbolizes solar energy and is used as decorations and as tea and salad ingredients. As with the spring equinox, the summer solstice has long been regarded by herbalists as an important time for gathering wild plants, so if green witchery is your path, consider including such harvesting as part of your yearly cycle.

Six weeks later comes the ancient Celtic fire feast Lughnasa or Lammas, the harvest or "first fruits" holiday celebrated on August 1. In old Ireland, this was the day when huge blazes, the "clairs," were set on hilltops. Cattle were driven between the fires to purify them, and lovers leapt over the flames in hopes of a fertile union. Today in County Kerry the Puck Fair is the oldest surviving Lughnasa ritual. There each August a wild goat is captured, crowned, elevated on a festooned platform, and lauded as king of the festival.

Goats on elevated platforms and herds of cattle driven between balefires will certainly gain the attention of neighbors, if not the national media, so less ostentatious outdoor Lughnasa celebrations are probably in order. As with Beltane, the fire pit is the center of the festival. If you have been clearing land, this is an excellent time for a brush burning—and, in fact, it's likely that the origins of such fire feasts are in the agriculturalist's need for efficient disposal of windfallen branches, trees cut to open new fields, and willow prunings.

Such prunings can be used to create a special and memorable Lughnasa festival. The Celts were said—by Julius Caesar, among others—to have burned huge "wicker men" filled with sacrifices—which, if it is true, may have included convicts, slaves, or other captives. Capital punishment may have returned to some states, but wicker-man burnings are still out of fashion. However, there is an important idea behind the image: to rid the land, and society, of useless or damaging elements, as well as to offer sacrifice in return for the plentiful harvest.

To adapt that ritual for contemporary use, craft small wicker boxes, fill them with emblems of what you wish to eliminate from your life, and burn them in the

Lughnasa blaze. Although willow is traditional for wickerwork, other shrubs and vines are equally adaptable. Grape vines or forsythia, for instance, can be trimmed of early growth in spring and the prunings twisted into little nests. Let them dry over the course of the summer and they will be suitable quick-to-ignite boxes for your sacrifice.

To denote the habit, force, or energy you wish to eliminate from your life, find a picture that represents it or an object that embodies it. Or write it—a single word will do, or expand it into a paragraph or an essay. If you wish to eliminate a bad health habit, for instance, burn a cigarette or a few cafeteria packets of sugar; should you wish to move beyond negative thinking, write a list of self-derogatory comments on a sheet of paper. Tuck the emblem or paper into the box and then, as you feed it to the flames, concentrate on the sensations of its destruction. Watch it grow redder, then burst into flame; watch the pattern of the smoke it emits. As you do so, imagine the end of the habits, thought patterns, or negative cycles you wish to eliminate.

Having released the negative thoughts, habits, or opinions, you are now free to replace them. Just as the seeds of many plants are given forth in late summer to rest underground until spring brings them forth, so Lughnasa is a good time to plant the seeds of what you wish to see develop over the next year. Again, do this symbolically: pass around a communion plate on which sunflower seeds and other nuts are arrayed, and have each member of the party feed another one, literally planting the seeds of renewal.

Should you have sufficient land to have a bonfire, be sure to take the practical precautions of checking the fire regulations and the weather conditions. In windy or hot weather, fire can spread rapidly. Avoid this by placing your bonfire away from other flammables, having water at the ready for dowsing, and planning to stay with the fire until it's thoroughly out. This time of year, sitting around a bonfire at night spinning yarns and singing songs is a traditional pleasure. Try it once and it will become part of your yearly cycle forever.

Fall Celebrations: Equinox and Hallowe'en

As leaves begin to yellow and release themselves into the wind, the yearly cycle of vegetation might seem complete. But the garden's cycle, like that of the year, includes dark seasons as well as light. There are seasons when the soil rests—when nature sleeps and prepares for a new spring. Part of the spiritual meaning to be found in the garden is the contemplation—nay, the embracing—of the parts of life that are so often negated by our culture. Age, barrenness, and rest are not highly valued in our youthful, productive, busy world. Yet without periods of sustained quiet, the soul does not mature, nor does the garden bear its fruit and flowers.

In the fall and winter garden we can begin to become more spiritually whole through contemplation, meditation, and ritual. Vital though the growing seasons are, they represent less of a spiritual challenge. Contemporary values support constant growth and expansion, not contraction and retreat. Thus, though using the garden for seasonal rituals might seem easier, more pleasant, in spring and summer, the minor inconveniences and potential discomforts of celebrating out of doors in fall and winter are offset by the spiritual lessons to be learned.

These begin with fall equinox, the time of letting go. The light and dark balance, briefly, on September 21 as they did on March 21. But in spring, the planet tips the next day toward the daylight, while in fall, that balance slides imperceptibly but inexorably toward darkness. Yet fall has its own splendid beauty, and the equinox is a time for memorable rituals in the garden. We find fewer traditional celebrations to base contemporary rituals on because, in subsistence communities, harvest was a busy time as the winter's food was gathered and stored. Celebration came later, after root cellar and granary were filled to bursting with the foods that would sustain the family during the long winter.

But in our more leisurely times, fall equinox offers the opportunity for a ritual acknowledging change and mutability. The perfect time for such a ritual is sunset, which is to the day as autumnal equinox is to the year. Begin the ritual by gathering around the fire pit a half-hour or so before sunset. Share foods that are condensed and refined: nuts, grains, apples drenched with honey. As you share them, reflect individually and as a group on the gifts the year has brought you, naming those gifts and thanking the universe for providing them.

Finish this communion as the sun approaches the horizon. As it does so, pass around a goblet filled with brandy or other refined spirits, absorbing the hot spark of the sun's fire that, captured in the grape or grain, has been distilled into its essence. Speak of the great ideals that move your soul, that guide your life. Share your dreams of the fullest, most profound life you can imagine. Speak of the dreams you hold for your relationships and your family. Describe the changes you hope for in your profession, education, or creative life.

At this time, when the seeds nestle into the heart of earth's cooling soil to burgeon again in spring, plant new dreams in your heart. It may be seasons, even years, before they rise and flower—but they can never come to fruition if they are not planted deep. Pour out some of the liqueur on the resting earth, then drink deep, deep, deep.

After the autumnal equinox comes one of the most powerful feasts of the ancient Celtic year—so powerful that it continues to be celebrated today, despite general ignorance of its original meaning. Hallowe'en remains the night when the veils between this world and the next are lifted, permitting visitations from unknown ancestors and loved ones who have passed into the summerland. To many of our forebears such visitations were not entirely welcome. The ancestors might need to be appeased for some unintended slight, and loved ones might draw those left behind over the boundary into the other world. With the understanding that spirits would not visit a home already visited, the elders dressed in outlandish attire and visited each home to inoculate it against spirit invasion—the tradition surviving in our contemporary trick-or-treating.

Hallowe'en was originally called Samhain, a Gaelic word meaning "summer's end." It's a powerful pivot point in the year. Light has decreased so substantially that the world now seems plunged into darkness; spring seems far away indeed. Yet this is also the time when harvest swells the barns. In the past, it was a time when newly butchered meat was still available in plenty, as the herds were culled down to just the number of cattle, sheep, and other animals that could be sustained over the winter. Thus there is an element of thanksgiving in the feasting of Samhain—giving thanks for fertile times past and praying for earth's favor in the times to come.

Samhain is one ritual occasion when outdoor ritual is easily performed, even for those with head-shaking neighbors. When everyone is dressing up like witches, who's to know the real ones? And nothing is quite so visually memorable as the vision of masked, hooded, and cloaked dancers around a winter fire. You may wish to perform some of your ritual indoors, both for privacy and for comfort, but plan to incorporate an outdoor bonfire as the climax of your celebration. Wear masks that invoke either animal totems or ancestral figures. As you dance, let them possess your body and move in the way they most desire.

A common Hallowe'en practice that has its roots in our gardens is the carving of jack-o'-lanterns. In Ireland and Scotland, turnips too big and woody to be used for food were carved in this fashion, each "head" representing a deceased ancestor or loved one. In the New World, larger and softer pumpkins were adopted for carving, but the somewhat ominous sense was never lost. Growing and carving your own jack-o'-lanterns ties you to old customs that mark the connection of this season with the "beloved dead."

Winter in the Garden: Winter Solstice and Imbolc

After the celebration of Hallowe'en, sunlight diminishes for another six weeks. Then comes the winter solstice, the year's longest night, the feast marked by ancient Romans as Saturnalia and celebrated by Christian believers as the birth of the savior. In all centuries and all traditions, the depth of winter is the time for a feast of hope for rebirth.

Winter solstice is, in many places, difficult to celebrate outdoors. The deciduous trees are empty of leaves, making for less privacy than at other seasons. Weather is usually uncomfortable and sometimes downright unpleasant. Best to celebrate this by an indoor hearth, in comfort and brightness.

Yet there is no scripture that says celebrations have to be held entirely outdoors or inside. And winter solstice is an ideal time to hold part of your ritual outside, where you can feel the tangy spark of winter, while the rest of it takes place near the yule log, whose glowing embers will be reflected in loved ones' eyes—like the sun that, though distant and diminished, is yet alive and strong, ready to return.

The year's longest night is, paradoxically, the festival of light. For when do we need light more than in winter's depths? Thus the symbols of the season are ones redolent with hope: the bright red berries of the holly bush and the silver ones of the mistletoe, promising growth in spring; the spruce and pine boughs, still green despite winter's chill; and the light of candles and hearth-fires, warming us despite the sun's long absence.

Even where winters are mild we suffer from the soul's winter, for the retreat—however slight—of sunlight signals our spirits that the time of withdrawal is at hand. At its worst this seasonal mood can be somber and even hopeless; at its best it is a time to reflect on what wealth we need to survive: the physical glow of the sun's energy, the emotional warmth of love, the intellectual fire of new ideas, the spiritual spark of grace. In summer, when all is growing, we have no time to ask ourselves how much, how little, we truly need. And in the commercial world of today's Christmas time, we rarely take time to ask ourselves how small a spark proves sufficient to nurture us through to the next period of growth.

In ancient days, when food was stored through the winter and spring was a time of enforced fasting because all but the seed-grain was gone, winter solstice was a final harvest feast. Vegetables and fruits that would decompose if kept longer were devoured with joy and delight. Similarly, meats that would begin to spoil were shared amidst song and story. We do not need to plan this way now, with our year-round seasonal delicacies. But with increasing awareness of the desirability of local produce, more people are returning to the foodways of earlier times. Even if you don't (yet) have a root cellar to store your potatoes and carrots and cabbages, you will find great satisfaction in eating squash and beans and apples at this time of year, leaving the tasteless, jetlagged strawberries and melons for others.

Contemporary solstice festivals should focus on how little, not how much, we need for happiness. Merchants have come to depend on the holiday trade. Often half of all the year's retail sales are made between Thanksgiving and Christmas. One way to honor the spirit of the season is to spend consciously, in a way that supports your ideals. Patronizing small merchants in your neighborhood, buying gifts from alternative or Pagan or minority mail-order firms, buying art directly from artists—these are powerful ways of making your gift dollar have significance.

You can as well or instead make gifts for the holidays. The garden is a rich source of possibilities: dried flower arrangements, honeyed jams, relishes and pickles, home-preserved teas and herbs, pressed and mounted leaves, berry vinegars, stewed fruits. A jar of homemade raspberry jam flavored with local honey brings the blessings of your summer garden into the winter months. You might consider preserves in a basket trimmed with dried herbs, a wreath with flowers from the eight major festivals, or a blank book decorated with your own photographs or sketches of the garden. Another garden gifting project is to annually decide on a "dinner party" package and grow the ingredients: peppers and beans for chili, tomato sauce and pesto for spaghetti. Such gifts are welcome reminders, in the dark of winter, of the earth's summer bounty.

Finally, you could hold a giveaway. Find objects in your house that you truly treasure but do not use. Invite friends to do the same. At solstice, exchange them: you might have the wrapped objects find their new owners through a grab bag, you might display them and let friends make their own selections, or you might determine in advance who will get what object. A small card giving the history and significance of the object can make it especially meaningful. Just be certain that the gifts for the giveaway are objects you genuinely value. If it should be thrown away, it's not for the giveaway.

The year's final festival occurs six weeks after the solstice. Light has begun to grow, but winter still holds us fast in its grip. The Celtic festival of Imbolc ("in the belly," representing the pregnancy of the cattle), celebrated on February 1, is aptly symbolized by the candles that give it its alternative name of Candlemas. Small lights against the darkness are appropriate to this midwinter moment, for though sap is beginning to stir in trees and plants are swelling slowly underground, the garden's surface is still barren.

Candles, symbol of the season, are of course appropriate for any outdoor rituals held on Imbolc. So, too, are sparklers, which can make an especially lovely sight against snow if you celebrate in a northerly or mountainous site. While it would be possible to use the fire pit at this time of year, it is symbolically inappropriate, for the fire of life is active in small flames only and is not ready to spread to a bonfire.

In ancient Ireland, Imbolc was the day on which the goddess was said to come forth from the underworld pregnant with the new life of spring. It was also the time when the year's crop of new lambs was born and so is also represented by the milk that nurtures the younglings. So, too, the milky sap rises in the trees. If you have maples or birches, you may wish to tap one, to provide a sweet, light drink for your chalice on this festival day.

In Ireland, where the feast is still celebrated, Imbolc is the feast of Brigit, triple goddess of the alchemical powers of smithcraft, poetry, and healing. In her honor, just-sprung-up rushes were gathered and woven into sun symbols called "Brigit crosses." You may have rushes appearing in your wetlands at this time of year, or you may find a similar grass that can be woven together. If you are in a more northerly climate, you can celebrate Brigit with the old tradition of the *bhrat brighde* (pronounced "brat breed"), or "Brigit mantle." Select a small tree or bush that is close to your door and protected from wind. On the night of February 1, secure a cloth on the tree. You can tie one corner to a branch, or use a clothespin or just arrange the fabric across the branches. The next morning, bring the cloth back inside. At dawn, Irish folk belief says, Brigit walks upon the cloth, filling it with her healing powers. Such a Brigit mantle can be cut into strips or left whole. It is used in healing ceremonies for the entire year.

Celebrating the Gardening Self

Thus ends the garden's year of celebration. The ancient cycle of the agricultural year is more meaningful to gardeners than to other contemporary Americans. Even without consciously celebrating these festivals, gardeners live in the rhythm of the seasons: seed catalogs in the depth of winter, like candles of hope; the frenzy and joy of planting; harvest rituals starring surplus zucchini; the sadness of finding the last soggy, overlooked cucumber in the fall garden. Marking the festivals is a way of making these connections conscious.

We have looked at ways of celebrating the seasons through noting the garden's changes. Lives, too, have seasons. We are born, we grow, we mate, we change our world through our actions, and then we pass on. Each of these passage points is traditionally marked with ceremony and ritual. And, whatever our religious faith, gardens provide setting and materials for rites of passage.

Three such rites are common throughout the world: rites of birth, of joining, and of death. Our lives today also offer many other opportunities for ritualizing personal changes. We may choose to celebrate the conclusion of an educational degree program or to mourn or even celebrate the end of a relationship. There are important birthdays and anniversaries, career transitions, culminations of special projects. All of these offer opportunities to gather with our community to announce and mark the change in our lives.

Many existing rituals can be adapted for life's passages. We have no lack of models for christenings and weddings and funerals, and birthday or anniversary celebrations often follow a standard model. Adapting these to the garden, however, sometimes represents a challenge. Some attempt to re-create an indoor environment out of doors. This often happens with weddings. Chairs are arranged as they would be in a church, the bride walks up the aisle on her father's arm, and—in perhaps the oddest feature of such events—the altar is decked with cut flowers. While such an event can be memorable, it fails to incorporate the garden as anything but a substitute for an indoor location.

Outdoor ceremonies of passage are far better when designed with the specific garden in mind, with the events emerging from a search for relevant personal symbolism as well as commonly accepted cultural symbols. So let us look at the process of designing such a ceremony.

In designing any ceremony, two factors must be considered: firstly, the individual (or family) symbol system; and secondly, the social symbols relevant to the occasion. The best ceremony is one mixing what is unique with what is expected, so that it is neither eccentric nor conventional. The following process, described through the experiences of real people, is useful not only for commonly celebrated life transitions like weddings but for individual points of change as well.

A *Divorce Ceremony*

For our first example, let us take a ceremony designed by a long-married woman who was embarking upon midlife as a single mother. Such transitions are often left unmarked, but this woman remembered many important ceremonies in her life, such as receiving a military commission and marrying her now-ex-husband, and the strength of those memories encouraged her to ritualize her new state. Designing a ceremony for divorce is, to some extent, easier than designing a wedding, for where there is no accepted symbol system, individual taste can reign.

First, the celebrant, working with a friend, brainstormed a list of words related to her new state. With her friend transcribing her words, she spoke as quickly as possible, editing out nothing—not even words that, like *hair*, seemed to have nothing to do with the purpose of the ceremony. A long list of words resulted, some of which represented false starts or irrelevant ideas. But among the words listed were the following: ring, fire, song, hair, dark, light, box, earth. Note that all are nouns; nouns and verbs most often provide the basis for ceremony, while adverbs and adjectives most often simply label or describe. Notice, too, that some of the words are opposite to others. Such tension often represents the truth of a situation, for human realities are rarely simple.

Knowing that these symbols represented her truest description of her state, the woman designed a ceremony that began indoors, in a darkened room with drawn curtains. Into this room, where her friends had gathered, she entered alone, wearing a black robe, her hair tightly bound atop her head. She stood before them and spoke of the pain of losing a relationship to which she had devoted many years. In the dim room, many tears were shed as the woman's pain became palpable.

Then, suddenly, music began. The woman moved to the fireplace, bent, and lit a fire, which had been carefully constructed to blaze instantly and dramatically. As she stood up, she loosened her hair, which fell down past her shoulders in a sudden sweep. She took off her dark robe to reveal a bright dress underneath.

At that signal, the curtains were suddenly pulled open, and light flooded the room. A member of the party began to sing "Turn! Turn! Turn! (To Everything There Is a Season)" while the woman removed her wedding ring, put it into a small box, and sealed that box with wax. The party then followed her to a tree, planted by the woman and her former husband, and beneath that tree she buried the ring that symbolized their union. Returning to the house, the now-celebrating group shared a meal and wine served by the woman, beaming with happiness at her new freedom.

A Rerooting Ceremony

Another woman, wishing to set down roots in a new city, invited several acquaintances to join her in ritualizing the change in her life. Brainstorming had revealed several words crucial to the change she felt: binding, new growth, and roses. Thus she began by showing photographs of her former home to her new friends. They then placed her in a chair in the center of the room. Taking several balls of bright yarn, they tied her into the chair, one string for each memory she named as binding her to her former home. Then, armed with scissors, they cut her loose—one string for each hope she had for her new life. They then accompanied her to the garden, where she planted a rosebush named for her new city, tying bits of the bright yarn to the stubby rose branches.

• • • • • •

The simple process of brainstorming words that describe the situation to be ritualized is the first step toward planning such an event. It is important that the brainstorming be free and unfettered by expectations and demands. As one can see in the first incident, the apparently irrelevant word *hair* created a particularly memorable moment in the ritual. Similarly, it is helpful to plan without regard for location and to let the garden's part in the event emerge during the planning process, rather than being determined at the outset. A mix of indoor and outdoor parts to a ceremony is especially effective if the ritual group is relatively small. For groups of twenty or more, movement between the two zones can be confusing and should be carefully planned.

Unique ceremonies such as those recorded above are to some extent easy to plan, both because there is no conventional format and because they are usually celebrated with a group whose worldview is congruent with that being ritualized. Weddings and funerals, however, present different challenges, for they bring together family members and others in the community who might feel confused or excluded by an entirely individual ritual. The planning process for such events, then, requires two parts: tapping into the individual symbol system and listing common elements to such rituals. Just as the individual list is then culled as the planners search for eloquent and appropriate actions, so the list of conventions is examined to determine which are appropriate. The exchange of rings, for instance, is a common part of wedding ceremonies; to some this indicates a tender gifting of each to the other, while to others it brings associations of materialism.

A Child's Funeral

The mix of expected and unexpected creates for the participants both a level of comfort and an attention to the inner meaning of the event. Thus, when a woman lost her young child in a tragic accident, a relatively conventional at-home funeral ended with a procession into the garden. As participants exited the house, they were given bright helium balloons—an image that had emerged in brainstorming. Standing in a circle in the garden, friends and family let the balloons go as the mother—her voice wringing with tears—said goodbye to her child. The circle of balloons slowly rose into the spring air, and the circle of mourners watched until every speck of color had disappeared. As they stared into the now-empty sky, every mourner vividly experienced the great vacuum the bereaved family faced.

• • • • • •

Such ceremonies are not only for the persons at their center, they are for the community as well. Like the ritual Hainuwele taught her people, they bind the human community through shared experience. For those to whom the garden is part of life, using the garden and its products in life's rituals is a natural expression of that connection.

Five

Gardens from Myth and Legend

Gaia

Of her I sing, the All-Mother,
old and rock-hard and beautiful.
Of her I sing, the nourisher,
she on whom everything feeds.
Of Gaia I sing. Whoever you are,
wherever you are, she feeds you
from her sacred treasury of life.
Bountiful harvests, beautiful
children, the fullness of life:
these are her gifts. Praise her.

. . . . . .

Homeric hymn to Gaia

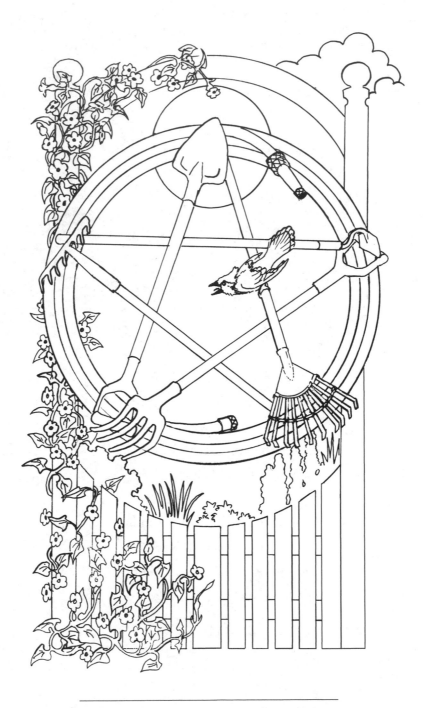

With every passing year, gardening has become a more popular hobby in America. Every year thousands of new gardeners discover the delight of savoring the first vine-ripened tomato, celebrating the abundance of strawberries even a small bed can provide, and filling vases with fragrant flowers from just outside the patio door. More experienced gardeners find increased access to plants, seeds, and supplies, as well as enjoying the access that the Internet brings to rare specimens.

Many gardeners, both new and experienced, focus their efforts on edibles. The locavore movement encourages people to eat from their own region and season-ally. Nothing connects you to your homeplace more fully than eating what is fresh and local, whether you grow it yourself or buy at a farmers' market or local grocery. Those involved in the earth spirituality movement are usually drawn to locavore eating, and locavores often find themselves becoming interested in other expres-sions of connections with the earth.

But gardens nourish more than the body. Throughout history, "pleasure gardens" have offered a feast for the eye and the spirit. These need not be large or expen-sive to create, for devoting a portion of the garden to meditation and contempla-tion of nature's beauty can be as simple as setting aside a corner with a bench and some flowers. The gardens that follow have been designed to inspire gardeners of all levels of experience to create tableaus in honor of earth's magical beauty. In some cases, suggestions for herbs or vegetables have been offered as alternatives to purely decorative plants. There is no reason not to mix edibles with decorative plants, and readers are encouraged to explore possibilities beyond what are offered in this book. But the gardens in this book were inspired by traditions of gardens whose purpose was meditation, ritual, or aesthetic enjoyment. Many fine books will help you design your vegetable garden, but few others focus on the nurturance of the soul.

Each of the following gardens honors a mythic figure. Many are designed around plants whose names or traditional uses reflect the myth or divinity. In most spiri-tual traditions, names are important, so in addition to color, height, and cultivation needs, the names of specific varieties have been chosen to enhance the garden's depth of meaning. Putting a Madonna lily in an Aphrodite garden might make aesthetic sense, but when appropriately named varieties are available, why not use them? Suggestions of named varieties are also made because, despite (indeed, because of) the vast number of options available online today, it can be extremely difficult to locate plants with appropriate names. Not only are there hundreds of options to sort through, but also an individual might not recognize potential acquisitions. In a list of fifty Japanese maples, not everyone would notice that Oto Hime is the name of the goddess of the sea, for instance. As always, the offerings are suggestions only; other plants could be substituted if the gardener requires or the site demands.

With each garden, legends and lore about the figures or myths that inspired it are provided, as well as specific plant and structure lists. Unless otherwise noted, the gardens are designed to thrive in zones 5 through 8—the temperate regions for gardening. Many plants mentioned survive in more extreme climates, but check with a local garden shop, botanic garden, or master gardener before planting if you live outside those zones. In addition, if you live in colder zones (1 through 4, from Alaska through Canada to the northern tier of the USA) or warmer (zones 9 and 10, including parts of California as well as the southern states), you can design your own versions of these gardens from the resources provided in the appendices. A list of providers of rare and unusual plants is found in appendix 1.

As you use or adapt these gardens, be sure that none of the plants are invasive in your area. In its natural terrain, every plant is kept in check by bugs that dine on it, weather that inhibits its spread, or some other natural mechanism. In a new place lacking these inhibitors, it may run rampant. The beautiful blooming rhododendron, for instance, is strangling the last stands of native Irish oaks, just as the Asian kudzu vine is overwhelming America's southern ecosystems. Almost every now-problematic plant was deliberately planted by a gardener who liked its shape or color, or occasionally by a scientist seeking to solve an ecological problem. Some invasives are still sold by nursery operators who are either unaware of the danger or unscrupulous enough not to care. But no pretty flowerbed is worth acres of despoiled natural land. Every region has readily available lists of invasive plants, so be sure to check them out before planting.

In all cases, remember to check soil and light conditions. Like most plants, those in these gardens require average garden soil. If you have especially heavy clay or very sandy soil, amending it with organic matter is necessary for the plants to thrive. Similarly, unless otherwise specified, the designs assume a relatively sunny location. If your site has heavy shade, try the Angel Garden (page 105) or the Sorcerer's Secret Garden (page 187).

Some of these gardens take their inspiration from European poetic gardens and Chinese scholar's gardens, with plants selected for what they represent rather than simply to attain a certain shape or color range. Other garden traditions form the backdrop of specific gardens in this chapter, such as the Japanese garden for Kuan-Yin and the sacred grove of Greek tradition for Artemis. All show the influence of contemporary garden practice, which acknowledges limitations on time for cultivation as well as a desire for gardens to be lived in, not just admired from a distance. Some of the great gardens of the past required paid servants or resident monks to maintain. The gardens in this book are designed so as not to require intensive care after planting.

After reading these plans and ideas, think hard about what you want, then create your own versions—or even something entirely different. Garden plans are like recipes. Even the most fabulous cake recipe needs to be tweaked for high-altitude cooking, humidity can affect the amount of flour needed for a perfect loaf of bread, and a cook's personal taste may call for more or less of an herb or spice. In the same way, these garden plans are not offered as unalterable directions but rather as inspirations. If you want to change them, do so, and enjoy the results!

These plans do not exhaust the possibilities of magical gardening. If you do not find your favorite divinity, festival, or mythic cycle, create your own garden plan around that theme. Plant a red garden for the fierce war god Mars, a summer solstice daisy garden, or a grape-covered Bower of Bacchus for the wine god. Erect a herm—a Greek boundary marker made of stone—at each corner of your property in honor of that patron of thieves and merchants, Hermes. Build a garden of Paradise after the Islamic fashion, with the waters of eternity crossing in its center. Plant a zodiac garden with flowers for each sign in a generous circle. Why limit yourself to a line of impatiens or a standard perennial border when you can create a garden that reflects your spiritual ideals as well as your gardening aesthetic?

Plants listed in this chapter are described by species name, followed by variety. All are available from suppliers listed in appendix 1. In most cases, the variety name is significant to the garden theme, so to duplicate such gardens, you'll need more than what your local garden center can provide. The substitution of similar, more common varieties is possible and even encouraged.

Finding specific varieties of plants has become far easier now that most seed and plant providers provide an Internet catalog. In order to make your search for these special plants easier, appendix 1 provides the addresses (both physical and websites) of nurseries carrying every plant mentioned in these pages. To make searching easier, the botanical name of each plant is provided in Latin beside the most common name. Using these botanical names makes Internet searching quicker and assures that you find the exact plant in question.

You need not create any of these gardens within one growing season. The gardens are all based primarily on perennials, which take from two to five years to reach their full growth. In planting, allow room for expansion, then be patient while the garden grows. Once established, your garden should give you many years of delight and inspiration.

Garden Inspirations

Creating a garden means more than just sticking some rose bushes in the ground and hoping they'll grow. Effective garden design requires not only knowing the horticultural needs of various plants but also how their various growth habits (height, color, bloom time) will interact with each other to create a pleasing and dynamic whole. It helps, as well, to learn something about the great traditions of garden design, especially those related to spirituality: medieval herb gardens, Islamic paradise gardens, Zen gardens, Chinese scholar's gardens. Each of these, and other garden traditions, teaches us about creating space that allows for reflective and creative connection with the earth.

One excellent way to expand your gardening vision is to visit established gardens, especially those devoted to spiritual or magical themes. Most regions boast botanic gardens or arboretums displaying a variety of theme gardens. Even in winter, visiting such gardens can provide inspiration, for many have greenhouse facilities and some gardens designed for the off-season.

The St. Louis Botanical Garden has a beautiful Chinese garden with moon-viewing windows and complex stone pavements, while the Chicago Botanic Garden offers visitors one of the most extensive and well-designed Japanese gardens in the nation. Another great Japanese garden can be found in Portland, also famous for its rose gardens. Near Austin, the Lady Bird Johnson Wildflower Center displays "garden rooms" designed entirely with native plants. In New York City, the Cloisters displays a fine example of a medieval herb garden that beautifully offsets the art of that period, also on display. In Montreal, an unusual version of the herb garden draws attention: a poison garden! (If you've ever wondered what belladonna looks like, here's your chance.) Over in the UK, a similar garden can be found at Alnwick Castle in Northumberland, which is familiar to many people as Hogwarts from the first two Harry Potter films. Resources for botanical gardens and arboretums can be found in appendix 4.

In addition to these public gardens, some designers have created gardens specifically devoted to spiritual or magical themes. Some of these gardens feature public educational events; others offer guided explanatory tours. Even if you can't visit in person, a virtual visit can inspire your creativity. Further information on these gardens can be found in appendix 4.

- In central Florida, the artist Iyanifa Vassa has created a series of gardens dedicated to the African powers honored by the animistic philosophy and religion of Ifa, from the Yoruba culture of West Africa. Called the Sacred Orisa Gardens at Ola Olu, these gardens range from an altar to Esu, messenger orisa of openings, that takes the form of a head emerging from the ground, to a large feather-crowned image of Osun, goddess of love and beauty. The grounds are open for visitation by arrangement only, as they are part of a retreat center devoted to honoring the Yoruba tradition.

- In Atlanta, artist and spiritual activist Shasta Zaring created a one-acre sanctuary to the divine feminine within the city's limits, creating an "urban wilderness" that uses no pesticides or herbicides so that butterflies, bees, and small mammals are sustained by its plants. When Zaring began her garden, the entire site was covered with invasive kudzu, but native and cultivated plants now thrive there. A Children's Garden and a goddess Medicine Wheel are among the garden's features, as well as a shrine to the Tibetan goddess Tara.

- In Los Angeles, as in many communities, a labyrinth forms the central spiritual symbol for the Peace Awareness Garden, which also has a meditation garden. The gardens, located near one of the city's major freeways, offer a respite from city energy with magnificent plantings and a paved labyrinth.

- In Ireland, an eleven-acre piece of land outside Galway City has been developed by Jenny Beal into the inspiring series of thematic gardens called Brigit's Garden, after the Celtic goddess and Christian saint whose festival is celebrated February 1. The centerpiece is four gardens with site-specific art and appropriate plantings that illustrate the four Celtic holidays. A goddess-shaped berm surrounds the Samhain garden, with its reflecting pond; the Imbolc garden includes a pavement showing Brigit's three phases, surrounded by spring-blooming fruit trees; Beltane's garden includes a gigantic bog-oak throne, approached through a line of standing stones; and the Lughnasa garden includes immense feasting tables surrounded by herb gardens. In the center of the gardens, a traditional roundhouse is used for educational events.

- In Cornwall, one of the most mythic places in England, the Eden Project was built into an abandoned clay mine; it is now a world-renowned nature center devoted to sharing ideas about sustainable living. An active arts program is also part of the project. Vast greenhouses sustain intensive plantings in the rainforest and Mediterranean gardens, and outdoor gardens include ones devoted to the myth and folklore of the region.

- In Italy, the famous Tarot Garden of artist Niki de Saint-Phalle centers on site-specific art related to the Major Arcana. Inspired by the architect Antonin Gaudi, Saint-Phalle created huge sculptures of the Emperor, the Magician, the High Priestess, and other familiar characters of the deck, which has historic ties to Italy. Recently, the Iris Sankey Arboretum in Escondido, California, created a similar garden dedicated to the myths of the region, including a huge mosaic throne for Califia, reputed goddess of the region.

Other spiritual, mythic, and magical gardens can be found, and more are being built every year. Visiting such gardens can inspire you to create your own special gardens once you return home.

An Angel Garden

One of the world's most famous outdoor rooms is the White Garden designed by the early twentieth-century artist Vita Sackville-West at her English estate, Sissinghurst. There, in the absence of bright floral tones, foliage textures and blossom shapes create visual interest. Such a garden comes into its own at night, especially when the garden is streaked with moonlight and the flowers shine with their own secret radiance.

Vita was a devil-may-care individualist, but she was an angel of inspiration to novelist Virginia Woolf—and to the thousands of gardeners who, following Vita's footsteps, have created their own white gardens. Thus this Angel Garden, a variation on the White Garden, is dedicated to her memory.

Perhaps all white gardens are angel gardens in disguise, their blooms recalling the feathered wings of these beings hovering between the divine and the human realms. For angels, in whatever culture they appear, are always messengers between these worlds. They bear the prayers of humans to the divine world, and they interpret to listeners the answers they bring in return. Some argue that angels have no actual essence—that they are the message itself, or at least that they cannot be distinguished from their messages. In such views, the winged radiant being our senses perceive is just the outward manifestation of the illuminating and uplifting message we receive.

Yet such abstractions do not satisfy our need to personalize the forces that are beyond us. And so innumerable names have emerged from the varying cultures—Christian and Jewish, Muslim and Zoroastrian—in which angels appear. Some angels are so well known that they provide familiar names for our children: Michael, Gabriel, Joel, and Raphael being among the most common. But the names of hundreds of others are recorded as well, from Meil, angel of Wednesdays, to Charuch, angel of the sixth hour of the day. Angels of special interest to gardeners include Abrid, angel of the summer solstice; Af Bri, angel of rain; Alpiel, angel of fruit trees; Makteil, angel of trees; Omael, angel of generation; Phorlakh, angel of earth; and especially Sachluph, the angel who controls the growth of plants.

Within this angel garden you may meditate on the many messages the flowers and green plants provide you. As you do so, listen to the whispering voices of other angels—and possibly the beating of their brilliant wings.

Locating the Garden

This garden is designed to surround a patio so that gardener and guests may best enjoy the blooms by day and in the serene moonlight as well. There are two repeating shade borders and one that demands sun; the arbor-entry border, too, requires sun. Although designed to completely surround an area approximately fifteen feet square, this garden can be adapted to any size, shape, or condition of shade. Simply repeat the borders as necessary, expanding the middle border area for a longer stretch.

Visitors enter this garden under a flower-shrouded arbor, which can be constructed on the site or purchased as a manufactured arbor. The arbor can be eliminated should the gardener wish to use this plan for a border or pair of borders. Or it can form the entrance to an Angel Pathway—perhaps leading to a little glade wherein an angel statue rests—created by repeating the design twice, with a two-foot space between.

This is one of those gardens that can be dressed up or down with sculptures, fountains, and other garden fixtures. Many suppliers provide angel sculptures for the garden, often replicas of historical ornaments: bas-reliefs of putti playing in the grape arbor, ornamental cherubs, kitschy angels on swings. You may wish to add one (please stop there!) such sculpture to the patio. The flowers alone, however, are angelic enough to sustain interest from spring through fall in this garden. The suggested plants are, as mentioned earlier, all white flowered in keeping both with the "white garden" movement and the tradition that angels are beings of white light.

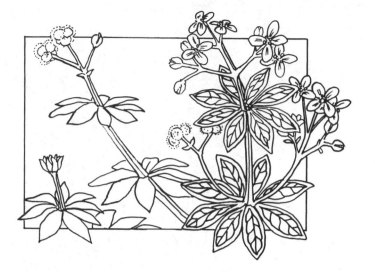

Planting the Borders

These deep borders are designed to bloom in successive white waves throughout the growing season, with the greatest concentration of flowers during the midsummer months, when outdoor entertaining is most likely to be enjoyed. Taller plants mass in the corners and at the center of each section, creating a scalloped effect.

The vine-covered arbor that serves as an entrance to the garden is planted with clematis and roses for a continuous display of flowers. The clematis is the stunning Marie Boisselot, with its pristine six-inch blooms. This clematis endures sun, so it mixes well with the rose that intertwines with it: the everblooming white Darlow's Enigma, a pure-white semidouble rose with rich perfume. The ancestry of this rare, hardy rose is unknown, but it performs well to zone 4, covering arbors with as much as twelve feet of canes.

At each corner of the garden, plant the tree peony called Renkaku ("flight of cranes"), whose tissue-soft white flowers festoon the small shrub late each spring. Unlike herbaceous peonies, this variety does not require staking. It grows slowly into a small shrub up to seven feet tall. Beneath the peonies, plant drifts of sweet woodruff (above), a groundcover that flowers in clusters of white stars in the spring. You may also wish to add some lilies of the valley here, although they can become invasive if not watched carefully.

In the center of the shadier sides of the border, place specimens of the giant Blue Angel hosta, whose huge heart-shaped leaves and white flowers make a dramatic garden statement. This hosta takes several years to attain its full growth, but don't cramp this magnificent variety. It grows as much as four feet tall and nearly as wide eventually. If you are an impatient gardener, you may fill in the space with white annuals or simply use an attractive mulch.

Surround the hosta with several astilbes of the variety Snowdrift, whose pure-white plumes appear midsummer on bright foliage mounds. In sprawling drifts on either side of the astilbe, plant the hardy native White Wood aster, whose starry blooms last throughout the late summer and fall. In front, plant several white bleeding hearts, whose delicate flowers arch over feathery foliage early in the season.

In the center of the sunny side, place a clump of the exotic but hardy hibiscus Blue River II, whose huge white blooms last much of the season. Named for the Oklahoma river where its parents were found, this hibiscus reaches five feet tall and four feet wide even as far north as zone 4.

Fill the sunny garden sections beside the hibiscus with mixed white lilies: Casablanca, the vigorous white Oriental lily with up to eight blooms per plant; White Butterflies, a June-flowering, arch-stemmed plant with many flowers; and of course White Angel, whose spectacularly pure-white flowers are lightly fragrant and bloom late in the summer.

Finally, surround the arbor with the white trumpet lily that is perhaps the best known: the Madonna lily. These candelabra of fragrant blooms light the way to the garden even in the purple evening. Underplant the lilies with spring-blooming bulbs: daffodils like White Ideal, the diminutive Angel's Tears, and the hyacinth L'Innocence. You may choose to strew these bulbs throughout the rest of the garden borders as well.

Should you desire a potted plant for this angel patio, consider the angel's trumpet, *Brugmansia* (see opposite page), a South American plant with huge, pendulous trumpets. Its dramatic appearance and delicate fragrance will certainly draw the attention of your visitors.

An Angel Garden

STRUCTURAL COMPONENTS

- arbor (manufactured or built to order)

- patio (any size or shape)

- angel sculpture, fountain, or other garden fixture

PLANT LIST

1. 1 Marie Boisselot clematis (*Clematis* 'Marie Boisselot'/ 'Mme. le Coultre')
2. 1 Darlow's Enigma rose (*Rosa* 'Darlow's Enigma')
3. 4 Renkaku tree peony (*Paeonia suffruticosa*)
4. 12 sweet woodruff (*Galium odoratum*)
5. 2 Blue Angel hostas (*Hosta* 'Blue Angel')
6. 8 Snowdrift astilbes (*Astilbe* × *arendsii* 'Snowdrift')
7. 12 White Wood asters (*Eurybia divaricata/Aster divaricatus*)
8. 8 Alba white bleeding hearts (*Dicentra spectabilis* 'Alba')
9. 1 Blue River II hibiscus (*Hibiscus* × 'Blue River II')
10. 10 mixed lilies: Casablanca (*Lilium* 'Casablanca'), White Butterflies (*Lilium* 'White Butterflies'), White Angel (*Lilium speciosum album* 'White Angel')
11. 10 Madonna lilies (*Lilium candidum*)
12. Mixed bulbs: White Ideal daffodil (*Narcissus* 'White Ideal'), Angel's Tears daffodil (*Narcissus triandrus*), L' Innocence hyacinth (*Hyacinthus orientalis* 'L' Innocence')

Optional: 1 angel's trumpet (*Brugmansia*)

Aphrodite's Bower

Aphrodite, the great love goddess, is completely at home in the garden. She is the very embodiment of what Welsh poet Dylan Thomas called "the force that through the green fuse drives the flower." Aphrodite—the magnetic power of attraction—is the sensual force that draws us together in ecstasy, the force that draws the pollinating bee to the open blossom.

There is nothing frivolous or flirtatious about Aphrodite's connection with flowers. However delicate and fragile they may appear, flowers are the reproductive organs of plants, petal veils between survival and extinction. The ancient Romans recognized this. They named one of their goddesses of sexuality Flora, the flower. She was honored in the festival called the Floralia (April 28–May 3), celebrated by naked women who scattered seeds and suggestively inscribed coins. Couples reveling upon the newly wakened earth were a happy feature of the annual celebration as well. Back yard kisses, ruled by Rome's kitchen-garden goddess Venus—who, though identified with Greek Aphrodite, was more flirtatious and coy than she—were only the opening act in the lustful drama played out in the gardens and fields of Italy.

In Greek myth, Aphrodite rules flower rather than fruit, passion rather than pregnancy. Thus it is appropriate that her garden is composed of flowers, flowers, and yet more flowers. This is not a garden of restraint and decorum. Like her primal energy, this garden should be abundant and exuberant. Let it be crowded and dense with bloom; let the plants touch each other and cry out to be touched. Let fragrances flood the air with perfume, especially on sultry summer nights. Let it excite all the senses, for this is a garden for lovers.

A throbbing combination of pinks and reds surrounds a small enclosure suitable for tender dalliances, an easy-to-erect structure shaped by eight posts in honor of the sacred number of the Babylonian love goddess Ishtar. The shape of the flowerbed recalls the generative power of the female, for this diamond or "lozenge" shape signifies the vulva in ancient Irish carvings. This also permits the garden to be tucked into a corner of the property, although it as easily could be isolated as an island in a lawn. Of the plants that have been selected for this planting, some are named for the goddess herself or for the powers she rules. Others have symbolic significance, and yet others have heart-shaped leaves or flowers appropriate to a lovers' retreat.

The Enclosure

Locate your garden in a corner of the property, its back wall almost touching the fence or property line, where you have room for a diamond approximately sixteen feet on a side. Make certain that the entrance to the bower does not face directly into another's sightline. This planting requires moderately good but not direct sun, so do not expect significant bloom if you place it in an extremely shady area.

The enclosure is simply formed with seven sections of prefabricated four-foot widths of latticework trellis. Erect eight four-by-four posts in an octagonal shape, sinking the posts in concrete and letting them harden at least overnight before completing the enclosure. Attach the trellises to the uprights, leaving an opening opposite the corner into which the bower nestles. You may wish to cover the trellises with fine-mesh screen, as the grapes that will cover them attract wasps and bees, which may limit your use of the enclosure.

At the base of all but the gateposts, plant the grape called Aurore. Named for the Roman dawn goddess whose appetite for pretty young men was legend, this pretty pink grape ripens early in September. The light white wine you can make from its fruit makes an appealing May Eve cup with a little sweet woodruff added (see information on this plant in the Angel Garden). After a few years, the vines cover the trellises, providing shade and privacy. Train the vines on wire over the top of the bower to create an entirely green outdoor room. Grapes can be rampant growers, so prune the vines late every winter.

On one side of the opening, plant the hardy climbing rose called Kiss of Desire. One of the most bountiful of all climbers, it blooms constantly, with huge red-edged white flowers set among deep green leathery leaves. Keep the rose trimmed sufficiently so that you won't accidentally enthorn a visitor's hand as it brushes the rose away to pass into the bower.

Within the enclosure, directly opposite the entry, place a statue of Aphrodite. Most cities have garden ornament centers where, among the concrete donkeys and gnomes and cherub fountains, you can find waist-tall renditions of the Venus de Milo or other classical depictions of the goddess. You can also find such statues available by mail order if you are not near a comprehensive lawn ornament center. Because of the planting of tall hosta beneath her, elevate this statue at least twelve inches. A concrete base, pillar, or an upended porcelain planter does the trick.

Along the sides of the bower, place two stone benches, and beside them, plant that extraordinarily fragrant wildflower lady's bedstraw. As its name implies, it was used in medieval times to stuff mattresses and emits a delirious fragrance when crushed.

Surrounding the elevated statue, plant the hosta named for Aphrodite (shown below). No matter how shady your bower may become as its vine covering extends itself, this sun-shunning plant will flourish. You'll appreciate the heady fragrance of its long-lasting, large white flowers in late summer. Its pale green leaves brighten the interior of your bower.

Simple grass could suffice for the floor of your bower, but it will need clipping frequently in early summer, and the bower's shape may frustrate your mower. A good substitute is a hardy fragrant herb that, once established, provides a fine cushioning floor. Lawn or Roman chamomile creates a lovely pineapple-scented carpet.

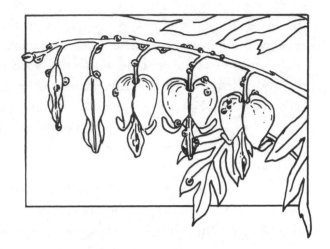

A low-growing mint—an herb bearing the name Mentha, a maiden goddess—is another good choice; the emerald crème-de-menthe-scented Corsican mint is especially nice. Pennyroyal, another mint, has the additional advantage of repelling insects. Bruised, these plants emit intoxicating aromas when walked on and thrive rather than suffer under such treatment.

The lawn or floral carpet extends through the bower's opening, encouraging visitors to enter and enjoy the green privacy within. Mass the areas beside the path with a traditional cottage-garden favorite, the bleeding heart (shown above), whose little red heart-shaped flowers point the way to your bower. The variety called Luxuriant has both the habit of exuberant growth and a name appropriate to your bower. Behind these, plant a short row of hardy chrysanthemum Venus, which burst into extravagant pink blossoms late in the year.

The Exterior Planting

The property line or fence behind the bower is swathed in pink French pussy willows (yes, the plant's name puns on Aphrodite's special glory). But in addition, willows are symbolically connected with sexual urges, perhaps because of their rampant habit of growth. The tender pink buds of the willow will grace your home altar during the spring and wrap the bower in a promising blush as well. Beneath these, plant the lovely rose-pink asclepias (butterfly weed) called Soulmate, a strong-stemmed perennial that attracts butterflies to your bower. Follow this planting with a row of Cytherea peonies. That flower, to the Chinese, represented the vulva, which is also recalled in the overall shape of the garden. The variety, which bears one of the names of Aphrodite herself, sustains huge, cup-shaped pink flowers.

At each corner of the diamond, plant the white pine called Venus. Although slow growing, these silver-blue conifers form a neat pyramid, symbolic of the female reproductive force. Nearer the bower itself, plant two Aphrodite azaleas, whose rosy midspring flowers illuminate this planting; in more northerly climes, replace these with the red-budded but white-flowered viburnum named for Aurora.

Plant the remaining area with the spiky red-flowered astilbe named Aphrodite. Their long bloom and easy habit of growth make these attractive lanterns, drawing the eye to the green bower. For early spring bloom, scatter within this patch—as well as among the mums and bleeding hearts—a variety of aptly named pink, white, and red tulips and narcissus: Love Call, Replete, Heart's Delight, Plaisir, Temple of Beauty, Beauty Queen, Angelique, and Passionale. Finally, edge the planting with the small heart-leaved hosta Happy Hearts, whose delicate white flowers provide a nice contrast late in the season to the strong spikes of astilbe.

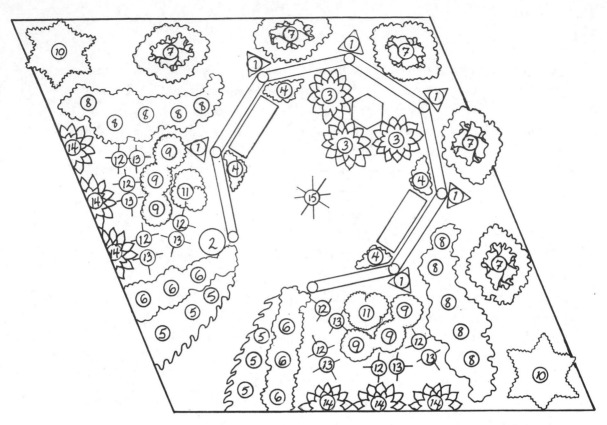

Aphrodite's Bower

STRUCTURAL COMPONENTS

- 8 four-by-four treated posts
- 7 two-by-four trellis sections
- concrete
- fine screen, if desired
- statue of Aphrodite
- concrete base, pillar, or large white-glazed pot
- 2 stone benches

1. 6 Aurore grapes (*Vitis* 'Seibel 5279')

2. 1 Kiss of Desire rose (*Rosa* 'Kiss of Desire', also called 'Harlekin')

3. 3 Aphrodite hostas (*Hosta* 'Aphrodite')

4. 4 lady's bedstraw (*Galium verum*)

5. 6 Luxuriant bleeding hearts (*Dicentra formosa* 'Luxuriant')

6. 6 Venus chrysanthemums (*Chrysanthemum rubellum* 'Venus')

7. 5 French pussy willows (*Salix caprea*)

8. 10 Soulmate asclepias (*Asclepias incarnata* 'Soulmate')

9. 6 Cytherea peonies (*Paeonia lactiflora* 'Cytherea')

10. 2 Venus white pines (*Pinus parviflora* 'Venus')

11. 2 Aphrodite azaleas (*Rhododendron hybrida* 'Aphrodite') or
Aurora viburnums (*Viburnum carlesii* 'Aurora')

12. 10 Aphrodite astilbes (*Astilbe simplicifolia* 'Aphrodite')
12 mixed daffodils and narcissus: Love Call (*Narcissus* 'Love Call'), Replete (*Narcissus* 'Replete'), Heart's Delight (*Tulipa kaufmanniana* 'Heart's Delight'), Plaisir (*Tulipa gregii* 'Plaisir'), Temple of Beauty (*Tulipa* 'Temple of Beauty'), Beauty Queen (*Tulipa* 'Beauty Queen'), Angelique (*Tulipa* 'Angelique'), and Passionale (*Tulipa* 'Passionale')

13. Happy Hearts hosta (*Hosta* 'Happy Hearts')

14. For interior cushioning lawn:
Roman chamomile (*Chamaemelum nobile*)
Corsican mint (*Mentha requienii*)
Pennyroyal (*Mentha pulegium*)

A Grove for Artemis
and an Artemisia Glade

Goddess of wildness and wilderness, Artemis is most at home in the untrammeled woodlands. Picture her there as the Greeks saw her: a wiry, strong huntress, stalking the land in the company of her equally athletic maidens. She races through the forest, quiver pounding against lithe back, feet bare and certain, lean hounds baying at her side, hunting for hunters less exacting than she is. Her arrows never injure young or pregnant deer, but she is swift and fierce in her punishment of any who would put opportunism before conservation.

She often hunts at night under the bright moon, which is part of her domain. Sometimes she stops at a crystalline spring, slaking her thirst in long gulps from cupped palms. Sometimes she slips off her simple garments and dives into the cool water, soon to be joined by her maidens. Woe betide the human who happens upon her then, naked and vulnerable, for she has been known to kill the insolent and leering. She is a private goddess, one never tamed, never confined.

So how can one build a garden to honor her? For those who have sufficient acreage, setting aside or planting a portion of woodland reserved for the goddess is appropriate. The urban or suburban devotee, lacking such expansive space, can still honor the huntress by building a glade filled with the fragrant herb that bears her name. In either case, land devoted to Artemis must not be overcultivated or planted in a regimented fashion. As the wild goddess, she is best honored in wild or nearly wild settings.

The Grove of Artemis

If you are already living in a wooded area, begin by familiarizing yourself fully with your land. The earth has many goddesses and gods, so do not assume that any wooded patch is by default the property of Artemis. Look for a true grove, one in which the trees, all of the same species, remind you of the band of nymphs who travel with the goddess. Even better is an area in which a mother tree is surrounded by her descendants. Should there be a pond or small spring in the grove, all the better to draw the tired huntress.

Such an area should be left undisturbed and mostly unaltered. No need to erect a marble statue of the goddess, for nature herself has provided a setting reflecting her maiden energy. Removing invasive undergrowth like buckthorn and honeysuckle that might hinder the free movement of a running troupe of nymphs is the only effort such a grove should take.

When visiting such a grove, be attentive to the birds and animals who make their homes there. Be the eyes and ears of the goddess, listening for the song of courting birds in the spring, watching for the signs of nesting and the tiny sounds of life's newest generation. In such meditations you have truly visited the temple of the goddess and encountered her abundant energy.

If you have sufficient land but no trees, you'll have a much grander project before you, for the establishment of a grove may well take longer than your current lifetime. Certainly it will be many years before saplings attain sufficient height to provide the kind of tranquil seclusion the goddess would appreciate. Should you wish to embark upon such a project, first familiarize yourself with the natural tree sequence of your area. Imported or specimen plants are inappropriate to this

goddess, whose grove should be of the trees that would naturally occur in the area. Select a species whose members naturally form groves. Oak is an excellent choice and evokes associations with Dea Artio, the Celtic form of Artemis, and most garden zones have one or more oaks that thrive in them. In higher latitudes or elevations, spruce or another conifer could form an especially charming grove for the goddess.

Purchase up to twenty trees from a reputable nursery supplier. Locate the approximate center of your grove, then set one tree just to the side of that spot. Arrange the remaining trees around the central tree, setting them sufficiently far apart so that they will not be crowded when they attain their mature height. Don't begin planting until you've settled on the arrangement of the grove, and don't be tempted to crowd the trees for more immediate impact. Impatience could cost a tree its life or health, and that would scarcely honor the goddess. After planting, be sure to keep trees well watered and fertilized for the first several years. With most trees, within a decade you will have a sufficiently well-grown grove to enjoy its Artemisian effect.

If your land would not naturally be wooded, an Artemis grove should not be attempted, for you do not honor this goddess by artifice. She can as readily be honored with a smaller theme garden in her name, such as that which follows.

The Artemisia Glade

For those with smaller spaces or ones ill-adapted to the establishment of a grove, an Artemisia glade is a happy substitute. This perennial plant is said to have so delighted the goddess that she named it after herself. It also goes by the common name wormwood, supposedly because the goddess used it in deworming her companion hounds. Most artemisias are somewhat silvery, white, or dull gray in tone, but heights and foliage shapes vary widely. Although some have noticeable flowers, most are grown for foliage shape and color rather than floral display.

A collection of artemisias allows for a complex play of textures in a monotone palette. Most adapt well to any sunny spot and provide a cooling note in the summer landscape. They are durable and long-lived perennials. Once established, your Artemisia Glade should be carefree: this plant's preference for dry heat means you

need not fuss over water requirements, and only an annual haircut is needed rather than extensive pruning.

Given the goddess's penchant for wildness, the Artemisia Glade should be established with plants liberally and naturally placed—no regimented rows here! Rather, drifts of similar plants should be encouraged to spread thickly. This garden is designed to tuck into a neglected spot in your yard. At ten by thirty feet, it is perfect as a side-yard planting or to replace a weedy patch at the rear of your property. Its dimensions can be readily changed to fit the space you have available, or this design could be converted into a border by eliminating the steppingstones through the center.

The first step is establishing the pathway. Use fieldstones or concrete steppingstones, available at most garden centers. The concrete steppingstones can be set right on the ground if it is level; fieldstones must be set into the ground to establish a firm pathway, preferably with a sand base. If you are building the garden around a side yard with an already-established concrete walk, consider breaking up the concrete with sledgehammers and removing some sections to ease the rigid formality of the pathway.

Next, establish the garden's outer boundaries with the taller artemisias. These plants rarely grow more than four feet in height, so this garden won't serve as a screen to the outside world. Should you desire more privacy, consider erecting a wooden fence at the perimeters of the garden. Stockade fencing or another plain variety is more in keeping with this goddess's energy than more elaborate fencing would be.

Along each shorter end of the garden, plant the white mugwort called Guizhou. This wiry, silver-filigree-leaved plant grows to five feet tall, quickly establishing itself as a focal point of the garden. While any lactiflora ("milk-flowered," for its panicles of white blooms) can be substituted, this Chinese variety adds a spike of color to the garden with its maroon stems.

Along the garden's longer sides, plant Big Sage artemisia, a sculptural accent plant whose fragrant silvery foliage adds another sensory dimension to your glade. Growing to four feet and spreading almost that far, this artemisia has twisting, contorted branches that create a dramatic evergreen hedge.

Beneath one planting of Big Sage, establish a drift of California sagebrush, a mounding shrub that grows to two feet tall and four feet wide. It cascades gracefully and provides a fine-textured note to the planting. On the other side, establish several small drifts of sand sagebrush (shown below), a small native shrub with airy, feathery foliage. Finally, fill in the remaining sections near the pathways with artemisias Silver Mound and canescens, both smallish perennials that, once established, create attractive mounds of silvery-gray feathery foliage.

Artemisias, once established, thrive and expand. You may find gardener friends with older artemisia beds they are willing to divide; you might substitute some of the above suggestions with gift plants of similar heights and shapes. You can't really mismatch artemisias, for the family demands similar culture and location, and the varieties of related foliage are invariably pleasing.

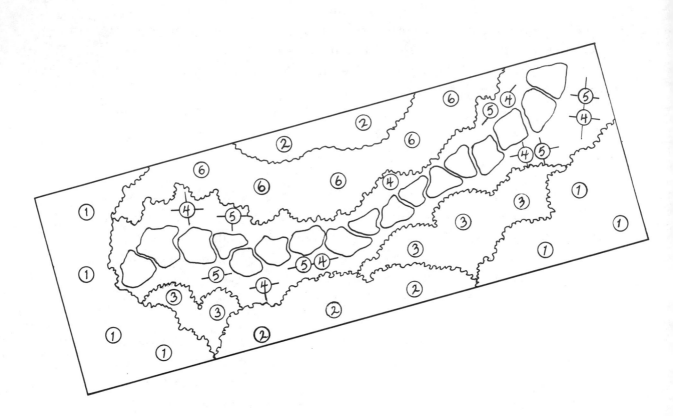

An Artemisia Glade

STRUCTURAL COMPONENTS

- up to 15 concrete steppingstones or fieldstones

Plant List

1. 5–7 Guizhou white mugwort (*Artemisia lactiflora* 'Guizhou')
2. 3–5 Big Sage artemisia (*Artemisia tridentata*, pictured below)
3. 3–5 Artemisia fifolia (*Artemisia filifolia* 'Sand Sage')
4. 7–10 Silver Mound artemisia (*Artemisia schmidtiana* 'Nana')
5. 7–10 Artemisia canescens (*Artemisia alba* 'Canescens')
6. 1 Montara California sagebrush (*Artemisia californica* 'Montara')

Bast's Cat Garden

Is there any magical cat lover who doesn't know of Bast, the cat goddess of ancient Egypt? At the vast pet cemetery near her city of Bubastis, embalmed pets in tiny cat-shaped mummy cases were buried by the thousands. Her shrines were decorated with magnificent sculpted cats, some wearing crystals in their foreheads, others decked with tiny golden earrings.

She was not only the ruler of feline life but also represented the healing life force to her worshipers. At her festivals, music and dance were important forms of worship. Her devotees believed that if they honored her with sufficient merriment, she would grant them long and healthy lives.

As a form of the sun goddess Hathor, Bast represented the gentle sun of the African winter, as opposed to her alter ego, the fierce lion Sekhmet, the scorching sun of summer. There are few myths about Bast, although Sekhmet is known for having almost destroyed humanity in a drunken rage. Bast, by contrast, is known best for the great festivals that honored her annually. Ancient writers were dumbfounded at the size of the events, for hundreds of thousands of people turned out to dance in honor of the cat goddess. Flotillas of rafts plied the Nile River in her honor, filled with jesting, singing worshipers of the goddess.

In more temperate climes, it is appropriate to honor the gentle cat goddess with a garden domestic cats can climb and play in—and find tidbits of catnip to stimulate their frolicking. It could also be built as a monument to one or more beloved and deceased cat companions.

Locating the Garden

This garden is not a traditional Egyptian one, for that would require limiting plants to those that grow in such warm climates as are found in American zones 7 and 8. Instead, this cat garden is adaptable to gardens in zones 4 through 7. Designed for a sunny corner of a fenced yard, this small garden includes a number of daylilies that demand good sun, so a west- or south-facing corner is best.

Bast's Plantings

Before beginning, build or purchase at least four planters suitable for mounting on your fence (or house wall). Hayrack planters, made of sturdy metal with removable peat plant holders, are especially suitable. But Bast is a whimsical goddess, so you could also consider gathering a variety of many-colored planters of different shapes. Mount these low on the walls so that the cats will have fun climbing them.

If you want to permit your own cats (and probably those of all your neighbors as well) access to the catnip, mount the planters—strongly—at staggered intervals approximately one cat-leap apart. Mints grow robustly even when frequently cut (or nibbled), so you will have enough at the end of the season to dry and stuff cat toys. Fill the planters with one or more varieties of *Nepeta* (catnip, *Nepeta cataria*, or the related catmint, *Nepeta mussinii*), such as Dropmore and Six Hills Giant, both of which have especially eye-pleasing foliage. The plants cascade over the edges and soften the corner with their pale blue flowers.

A little offset from the corner, plant a small tree or shrub—one that will *not* have berries, which would attract wild birds into the mouths of your cats. You also don't want a shrub that has too-tempting bark, which might encourage cats to kill it by scratching. The answer: a rosebush filled with yellow flowers in honor of sunny Bast. David Austin's old garden roses include several that would be suitable, such as pale yellow Blythe Spirit and the shrubby Golden Wings. In front of this specimen, plant several mounds of cat thyme (*Teucrium marum*), a clumping perennial herb related not to thyme but to germander, and which some cats prefer to catnip.

If you wish, you can place a small cat sculpture or two beneath the cat thyme, whose foliage almost hides them. Many museums have replicas of Bast's own image, some suitable for outdoor exposure. Cement or unpainted metal statues usually need no waterproofing but should be brought indoors in winter. Statues of other materials should be thoroughly waterproofed and carried indoors during harsh weather. Such decorations are optional, for your own cats or the rays of the sun can sufficiently represent the goddess.

In groups of five throughout the rest of the garden, plant daylilies with appropriate names: rich amber Egyptian Spice, violet Nile Plum, rosy Rahotep. These arch nicely over the edge of the lawn and provide a tangle of foliage through which cats can enjoyably stalk.

Note that gardens for pets must be carefully planned, as many plants are toxic to pets, which is why this garden is limited in range. Common plants toxic or potentially toxic to cats include aloe, amaryllis, azalea, baby's breath, begonia, buttercup, calla lily, carnation, castor bean plant, chamomile, daffodil, eucalyptus, foxglove, geranium, garlic, hibiscus, iris, lily, lily of the valley, morning glory, nicotinia, peony, rhubarb, sweet pea, tobacco, and tulip. Note that lilies are toxic to cats, but the daylilies that make up the bulk of this planting are a different species and are nontoxic.

It is worth considering roofing and walling this small garden with chicken wire or similar fencing. Songbirds are currently suffering from predation by housecats, to the point that some have become endangered. You want your cat companion to enjoy the outdoors, but do you want to be responsible for further devastation to the songbird population? Creating an environment that is friendly to both cats and birds is a good way to honor the goddesses of both species.

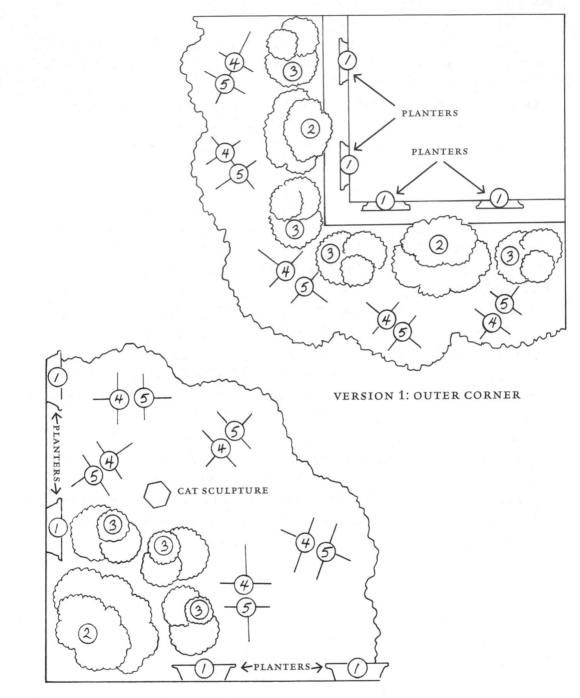

PLANTERS

PLANTERS

VERSION 1: OUTER CORNER

PLANTERS→

CAT SCULPTURE

←PLANTERS→

VERSION 2: INNER CORNER

GARDENS FROM MYTH AND LEGEND

Bast's Cat Garden

STRUCTURAL COMPONENTS

- 4–8 planters for catnip, plus secure wall-mounting apparatus
- cat sculpture (optional)

PLANT LIST

1. 10–15 catnip or catmint (*Nepeta cataria*) in various varieties, such as Dropmore (*Nepeta musinii* 'Dropmore' or *Nepeta faassenii* 'Dropmore'), Six Hills Giant (*Nepeta* × 'Six Hills Giant'), and Siberian catnip (*Nepeta siberica*)
2. 1 rose bush (*Rosa* 'Blythe Spirit' or 'Golden Wings')
3. 3 clumps cat thyme (*Teucrium marum*)
4, 5. Daylilies, approximately 7 each: orange/yellow Egyptian Spice (*Hemerocallis* 'Egyptian Spice'); purple/red Nile Plum (*Hemerocallis* 'Nile Plum') and Rahotep (*Hemerocallis* 'Rahotep')

The Royal Circle:
A Camelot Garden

Arthur, Guinevere, Lancelot. Merlin the magician. The Lady of the Lake, the Lady of Shalott. Gawain and Percivale. Tristan and Isolde.

How these names ring in our ears, even today, fifteen hundred years or more since their stories were first told! The story is too complex to tell in just one chapter and is known in many variants. All center on King Arthur, who holds the throne with the help of magical powers (Merlin and the fairy queen, the Lady of the Lake) and who married the beautiful and much younger Guinevere. Arthur surrounded himself with heroic knights, one of whom—the fine Lancelot of the Lake—won the eye and finally the heart of Guinevere. Despite the lovers' attempts to remain true to the king, their love ultimately doomed them. Meanwhile, Arthur's rejected son rose up in battle, and the promise of Camelot was ruined in war. Arthur was not killed but disappeared beneath the lake whose lady took him to her other-world, perhaps to come again when the time is right.

There is perhaps not a single myth that has inspired so much art, literature, and music than the cycle of stories of the Round Table and Camelot. Beginning with the Middle English *Le Morte d'Arthur* and *Sir Gawain and the Green Knight*, countless works of art have been created and countless artists have been drawn to the complex cycle of stories of love, betrayal, and magic. Such great works as William Morris's "Defense of Guinevere" and T. S. Eliot's "The Waste Land" have all relied on the "Matter of Britain," as the Camelot cycle is called. Painters, especially late Victorian artists like John Waterhouse, Dante Gabriel Rosetti, and (again) William Morris, were moved by the tragic story and painted scores of memorable versions of it.

The fascination has not waned, as attested by the phenomenal popularity of Marion Zimmer Bradley's novel *The Mists of Avalon* and of Loreena McKennitt's melodious setting of Lord Alfred Tennyson's poem "The Lady of Shalott." Movies such as *Excalibur* and *First Knight* bring the legends to cinematic life. And, of course, there was the musical (and later movie) that gave its name to the John F. Kennedy presidency in the United States: *Camelot*, that "one brief shining moment" for "happy-ever-aftering."

Although part of the cycle's resilient popularity rests in its psychological complexity, its archetypal truth is even more likely to account for the hold it has on us. Camelot reflects the organic process in which great possibilities are seeded, grow, and flourish, but must die in order for new life to emerge. It is an inevitable story, as inevitable as the garden's annual cycle of bloom and fruitfulness, death and rebirth.

A Round Garden for the Round Table

This garden requires an area of approximately twenty-five feet in diameter. Because its major plants prefer a sunny location, you may wish to locate this garden as a central island in your lawn, away from surrounding shade trees.

To symbolize their equality, King Arthur arrayed his knights around him at the Round Table, with none sitting at the head, none at the foot. Thus it is fitting to make your own private Camelot circular, its perimeter marked by a generous scalloped border of tall flowering larkspur (see opposite page) named for some of the major characters in the drama—King Arthur (royal violet with white), Guinevere (pink/lavender with black center), and Galahad (white). These lush, bright-toned perennials create a hedge as they shoot up annually to as much as six feet tall. If you stake the taller ones, you'll increase the sense of privacy within the circular garden.

The garden is designed for a flat surface, but if you have a slight elevation to situate the garden on, so much the better. Creating an artificial mound of topsoil, no more than three feet higher than the original soil, would also be appropriate. Glastonbury Tor, the steep-sided English mountain topped by its distinctive tower, is held by many to be the Isle of Avalon, the mythical island of apples to which Arthur is said to have been spirited upon his death. Building this garden on an artificial or natural mound would make it especially charming.

The circle is not the only geometric figure appropriate to this myth. The triangle—representing King Arthur, Queen Guinevere, and that peerless knight Lancelot—is equally appropriate. Thus, within the circle formed by the delphinium hedge is a triangle of shrubs. On one side of the path that curves into and out of the garden is a crabapple named Lancelot, an especially apt choice for the garden because of its connection to Avalon, isle of apples. The small tree covers itself with showy white blossoms each spring, which turn into mellow golden fruit that last

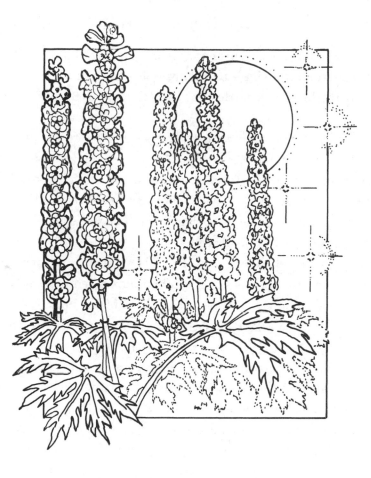

into the winter, drawing birds to feast upon it. Underneath the tree, place a small bench so that you may hide within Camelot's borders to meditate on love, probably, and perhaps loss and betrayal as well.

Across the path, to represent Arthur and Guinevere, plant two Lady of Shalott roses, named for the fairy woman who, cursed to weave forever in a tower, saw Lancelot and was lured to her death by his beauty. Bred by the famous British rose specialist David Austin, this rose is more robust than her namesake, for she blooms with orange-red chalice-shaped blossoms throughout the summer.

Select one rosebush to represent Arthur and place a large boulder next to it to recall the stone in which the once and future king found his famous sword Excalibur. Behind that bush, drag into position an old log, a dead tree, a large piece of driftwood, or a similar object. This serves as an emblem of Merlin, who was imprisoned in a tree—or, in variant legends, in stone—by his possessive mistress Vivienne. Situate the Merlin log so that it is close to Arthur's bush, as though protecting it.

Between the crabapple and the roses, build a path winding outward to the garden's borders. In addition to providing access to the garden's center, this path represents the river flowing by Arthur's castellated city of Camelot that the Lady of Shalott floated down, singing as she died for love of Lancelot. Although a path of woodchips or mulch would be acceptable, a better choice would be pebbles, creating the impression of a dry streambed.

Line the path with the hosta named Camelot, which provides a dark bluish-green border to reflect the blues of the delphiniums. Behind that border, scatter a combination of daffodils for early spring color: Merlin, a pert small-cupped daffodil with a red-banded yellow cup; Avalon, a large-cupped sturdy flower of buff yellow; and Camelot, a long-lasting clear yellow favorite.

Behind the Lancelot crabapple, place several patches of Royalty hosta, whose substantial mounds add their purple flowers to the garden in late summer. Behind them, and in a parallel area on the other side of the garden, plant drifts of the blue lungwort named Excalibur (pictured below), after Arthur's magical sword. These silvery mounding plants with their dark-green margins bloom blue-violet in the spring.

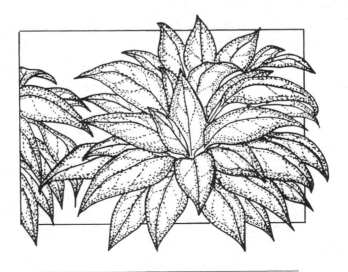

Finally, between the lungwort and the delphiniums, place a mixed drift of day-lilies whose names are connected to the Camelot cycle and whose colors resonate with the other purples, blues, and dark reds of the garden. Isolde is a dark purple daylily with a green throat; the plant's name recalls the myth, parallel to that of Arthur, of the fated love of Tristan for Isolde, promised wife of King Mark of Cornwall. Court Magician is a daylily honoring Arthur's magical advisor Merlin; it is rich purple with a chalky-lavender eye.

If you choose to build an artificial tor or use a natural rise for this garden, reverse the placement of the lungwort and the daylilies so that the lilies are not in deep shade between the hill and the delphiniums.

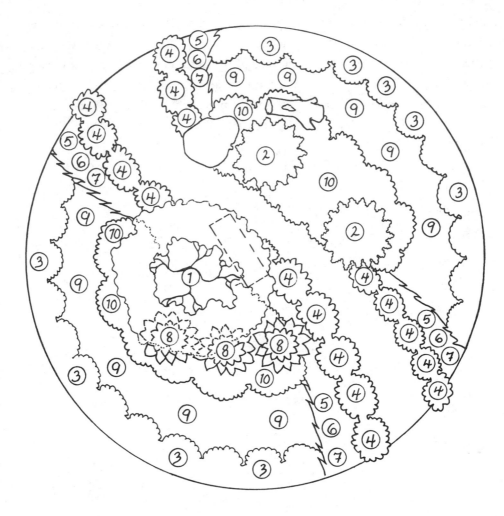

A Camelot Garden

STRUCTURAL COMPONENTS

- bench, preferably of stone
- boulder, at least 18 inches in diameter
- log, dead tree, or tree stump
- river pebbles for path

PLANT LIST

1. 1 Lancelot crabapple (*Malus* 'Lanzam')

2. 2 Lady of Shalott roses (*Rosa* 'Lady of Shalott')

3. 40 mixed larkspur: King Arthur (*Delphinium* 'King Arthur'), Galahad (*Delphinium* 'Galahad'), and Guinevere (*Delphinium* 'Guinevere')

4. 20 Camelot hostas (*Hosta* 'Camelot')

5. 24 Camelot daffodils (*Narcissus* 'Camelot')

6. 24 Avalon daffodils (*Narcissus* 'Avalon')

7. 24 Merlin daffodils (*Narcissus* 'Merlin')

8. 3 Royalty hostas (*Hosta* 'Royalty')

9. 10 Isolde daylilies (*Hemerocallis* 'Isolde'), 10 Court Magician daylilies (*Hemerocallis* 'Court Magician')

10. 20 Excalibur blue lungworts (*Pulmonaria* 'Excalibur')

A Grass Garden for Ceres

The ancient Romans did not have a single earth goddess. They had two. One was Tellus Mater, "Mother Soil," the rich, nurturing earth that sustained plant life. The other was Ceres, the force of vegetative growth—a goddess whose name we still use to represent one of the most important of her gifts to us, cereal grain.

Ceres was celebrated annually in a spring festival called the Ceralia, when foxes were set loose to run wildly through the Circus Maximus in central Rome with torches tied to their tails. Why foxes? Why torches? The meaning of the ritual either was not recorded or has been lost, but as fire often symbolizes vitality, while foxes are fire-colored, the rite suggests stirring up Ceres's vital forces to encourage an abundant harvest.

Ceres was called the "mother of cultivation" by the great poet Ovid, who noted that the best way to honor her was with her own seed-grain mixed with the entrails of a pregnant cow. Translated into contemporary gardening practice, this suggests a grass garden whose soil has been enriched by a substantial addition of organic fertilizer. Indeed, it is very close to some of the practices of biodynamic gardening as created by the sage Rudolph Steiner, who also established the child-cherishing Waldorf Schools.

To remind the goddess of her ancient ritual, you don't need to bother with foxes or torches. Use sparklers instead—just remember to wave them about the garden on April 19, the ancient feast day of Ceres, cheering on the goddess's efforts as you do so.

Establishing the Grass Garden

To most Americans, grass is the stuff of lawns. Monotonous even when well maintained, annoyingly weed- and pest-prone, our private lawns now cover more than thirty million acres—and that doesn't count the greens of golf courses, college campuses, and corporate headquarters. Whole aquifers are depleted to keep up with the required watering. And pets, along with pests, are regularly poisoned by the toxins necessary for this manicured look.

Ceres would shake her head. Lawns are useless, she would think. And she would be right—for they were designed to be. In times when even the smallest fertile

patch was necessary for food production, acreage set aside as lawn was a clear statement of conspicuous nonconsumption. (Lawns, please note, are quite distinct from
pastures. If fertilizer-producing four-legged mammals are the groundskeepers, it's
not a lawn.)

Our lawns are carpets of thwarted plants. The sole intention of a plant's exis-
tence is to create more plants: to flower, to attract bees for fertilization, to go to
seed. And what do we call a badly kept lawn (or person, for that matter)? Right:
seedy. No wonder Ceres is offended.

Thus this small garden is a peace offering to the goddess of grain, for the grasses
in it are intended to go to seed. Indeed, a great part of their beauty comes from the
sculptural effect of the seed heads, with their tiny wirelike protective filaments and
airy, dancing pods. Grass gardens are all-season beauties, for the tan, silver, and gray

stands of stiff stalks provide winter interest when little else is available to remind the gardener of springs and summers past and to come.

Grasses do not like wet feet, so this garden is placed on a raised bed filled with a mixture of compost, garden soil, and sand. If you have a well-drained area of the garden that receives full sun, you may not need to build such a bed but can plant the grasses directly into your garden soil.

Select a site with good sun. Especially good is a site where early morning or late-afternoon sun shines through the grasses, emphasizing their delicate forms. A breezy spot is also good. Not only do grasses stand up well to wind, but the movement of their seed heads is part of their graceful charm.

Plant the grasses in clumps, sufficiently far from each other so that their individual forms are distinct. Once you have installed the plants, cover the soil with a thick mulch of light-colored river pebbles. This provides even more visual distinction among the grasses as well as keeping down competing weeds. If weeds are a problem in your garden, you may wish to under-mulch with a thick padding of recycled newspaper.

Once established, grasses need little care. Most importantly, they need little extra water beyond what occurs naturally, except in severe drought conditions. Each spring, before new growth is seen, shear the clumps to four inches. Every three years, divide your grasses and extend the planting or endow your friends. You can add the fresh grasses to bouquets of garden flowers; dried, they are useful for wreaths, arrangements, and other decorations.

Grasses for Ceres

The grasses selected for this garden are hardy to zone 5, but many other grasses are available as substitutes, so you should be able to find grasses that thrive in your area. To design with substitutes, you need not follow the pattern set out here. Just keep in mind several principles of design: include grasses of varying heights and shapes but of compatible coloring (most grasses blend with each other well, so this is relatively easy), plant in drifts (no fewer than three plants set in a natural, non-linear pattern) rather than in regimented rows, and leave sufficient room for these perennial grasses to spread without crowding.

As an alternative, you may wish to establish a wild grass garden, especially if you live in a place where foxtails, wild asparagus, and similar plants grow readily. You may find an area on your property where some grasses are already growing. This suggests that the area has the right mix of soil and sun for a successful grass garden. For the next several years, weed out competing plants and wildflowers until you have only drifts of native grasses for Ceres's (and your) enjoyment. If no native grasses have volunteered for your garden, gather seeds in fall and distribute them immediately into your prepared soil. Again, use the basic design principles in establishing the general outline of the garden.

If you live in the Midwest, where prairie was once the predominant ecosystem, you may wish to establish a prairie. Prairie grasses such as big and little bluestem (*Andropogon gerardii* and *Schizachyrium scoparium*) and the charmingly named sideoats grama (*Bouteloua curtipendula*) have deep roots, the better to survive the droughts that are common on the plains. In the past, they would have maintained their dominance over invasive plants like garlic mustard (*Alliaria petiolata*) and purple loosestrife (*Lythrum salicaria*) through fire. Prairie fires would kill the shallow-rooted invaders, leaving the native plants to thrive. Today, throughout the Midwest, hobbyists are restoring native prairie through regular burning. If your land is not large or private enough for burning, consider joining a group through a university or nonprofit that burns prairies. It is an invigorating spring (and sometimes fall) ritual that restores land and the species that depend upon fire.

In our sample garden, the corner is anchored by tall, native switch grass, whose metallic blue seed heads rise to almost five feet and last well into winter. On the other side of the garden, curving fountain grass pours its rosy plumes over the garden's low supporting walls. Native to Asia, it is an especially pleasing grass in bouquets, fresh or dried. Beneath it, a drift of miniature fountain grass echoes the curving shape of the larger variety with its heavy midsummer blooms.

In the garden's center is a triangle of bluish wheat grass, notable for its self-renewing leaves. Corner clumps of mosquito grass add a delicate, ever-moving iridescence as short-stemmed seed heads dance above dense leaves.

Some possible substitutes for the switch grass are maiden grass—a shimmery, open fountain of silky grace—or feather reed grass, which grows up to seven feet tall with plumes of rose and buff that dance in the slightest wind. Fountain grass substitutes include any of the more than fifty species of tufted hair grass, with its undulating seed heads above neat, leafy mounds. For the shorter grasses in this garden, consider substituting sedge, dwarf miscanthus, deer grass, or moor grass.

A Grass Garden for Ceres

Plant List

1. 3 Heavy Metal switch grass (*Panicum virgatum* 'Heavy Metal')

2. 3 fountain grass (*Pennisetum setaceum*)

3. 3 blue wheat grass (*Elymus magellanicus*)

4. 3 mosquito grass (*Bouteloua gracilis*)

5. 5 Little Bunny miniature fountain grass (*Pennisetum* 'Little Bunny')

To substitute:

For Switch Grass: Any of many taller varieties of miscanthus/maiden grass, including Morning Light miscanthus (*Miscanthus sinensis* 'Morning Light'), a five-foot, silvery-white variety; or feather reed grass (*Calamagrostis* × *acutiflora* 'Stricta').

For Fountain Grass: One of the several varieties of *Deschampsia*, including Bronze Veil (*Deschampsia cespitosa* 'Bronzeschleier'), a golden-bronze variety; or Scottish hair grass (*Deschampsia cespitosa* 'Schottland'), with its four-foot-tall soft flower heads.

For Shorter Grasses: Many grasses can be substituted, among them golden carex (*Carex elata* 'Bowles Golden'), a rounded, yellow, compact grass; Adagio maiden grass (*Miscanthus sisnesis* 'Adagio'), a pink-panicled dwarf; Nippon maiden grass (*Miscanthus sisnesis* 'Nippon'), a reddish dwarf; purple moor grass (*Molinia caerulea* 'Strahlenquelle') or the thin, arrow-flowered mist grass that dries well (*Muhlenbergia capillaris*).

Two Dragon Gardens

Central Africa was terrorized by the mokèlé-mbèmbé, Ethiopia by the dragon of Silene, Italy by the tatzelworm, France by the peluda and tarasque. In Scandinavia, Fafnir struck fear into hearts, while England was terrorized by the Mordiford wyvern and the Lambton worm.

Dragons and dragon deities are found in the mythology of every continent, from Australia (where the bunyip reigns) to subarctic Canada (where we find tales of dragon-whales). Sea lizard, dragonet, basilisk, amphipter, pyrali, sirrush—these are some of the names given to this fierce and often fearsome figure. Its form is almost as variable as its name, for it appears winged and wingless, serpentine and footed, with a huge tail or none at all. Whatever its form, the dragon is acknowledged the world over.

The culture to which the dragon has been most symbolically important is that of China, where ancient emperors reserved for themselves the right to display the image of the five-toed dragon, while their attendants could claim only the four-toed. Ancient China saw the dragon as a complex creature with the head of a camel, eyes of a demon, horns of a stag, a cow's ears, a snake's neck, and a clam's belly. Its feet were those of tigers, its claws those of eagles, and its 117 scales were those of a fish: 81 of them beneficial, 36 malignant. A creature of earth, water, and sky, the dragon's special role was as intermediary between and among these parts of the cosmos.

A Chinese dragon lived an incredibly long time. Perhaps three thousand years passed from the time one hatched from its multicolored egg to its impressive maturity. The dragon passed through many stages, living as a water snake when young, then growing a carp's head and becoming a fish for almost a thousand years. It took another five hundred years to grow stag's horns on its head. Lastly, its branching wings thrust out, taking more than a thousand years to do so.

Once mature, a dragon could take on one of many possible tasks. The ti-lung protected streams and rivers. The fu-ts'ang lung guarded treasure. The yu lung helped mortals pass examinations. A few were given especially important tasks, such as that of the Yellow Dragon of the River Lo, which unveiled the trigrams of the I Ching to humankind.

In Europe, the dragon appears as a powerful creature with whom combat is the ultimate test for a hero. While some claim the dragon is a symbol of evil, less dualistic thinkers have interpreted the dragon's mythic role as that of "guardian at the gates," protecting spiritual secrets from those not strong enough or not yet ready to understand them. Thus St. George slaying the dragon becomes an image of a hero conquering his own weaknesses and fears in order to enter a greater spiritual initiation, rather than an emblem of right's might.

Why a dragon garden? Why invite this fierce being to your doorstep?

There are two reasons to consider adding dragon energy to your garden. Firstly is the dragon's connection with the forces of underground power, especially underground water. Secondly is the dragon nature of gardening itself, for in encountering the willful ways of our gardens, we encounter the lessons our spirit needs to learn. Every gardener is, to some extent, St. George slaying the demons of pride and grandiosity, of carelessness and excessive control. A dragon garden thus makes visible the soul's struggle with itself that is the essence of conscious gardening.

In welcoming the dragon into our gardens, we honor the generations of gardeners who have struggled with the energies of the earth and have learned from that struggle.

GARDENS FROM MYTH AND LEGEND

Design I: A Spiral of Trees

It is especially appropriate to center a dragon garden on trees, for these long-lived woody plants have symbolic meanings similar to the dragon itself. The tree, like the dragon, is a being of many levels: its hidden roots are deep underground, and its trunk points upward into the sky. Like the dragon, the tree partakes of the three levels: below, middle earth, and above.

Spiraling in to its central tree, a stunning dragon's-eye pine, this garden grove should be placed in a sunny, open part of your property. As the shrubs and trees mature, they provide substantial shade as well as a secret meditation spot where you can encounter your own dragon energy. You will need a space that is between forty and fifty feet in diameter to make both trees and gardener happy. Place this garden where you wish to eliminate an unattractive view, where you wish to provide more privacy, or where you want a deeply shaded retreat for oppressively hot days. Note that this, unlike most of the gardens in this book, requires a warm climate, as most of the trees are not hardy beyond zone 6.

The tree that forms the center of this garden grows to a significant height, perhaps sixty feet within twenty years. The trees and shrubs that spiral out from it diminish in height to small shrubs at the garden path's entry. Thus, as you follow the short path into the garden, you have a sense of entering a forest of increasing depth and mystery. At the spiral's center, place a bench or several rustic chairs to encourage meditation and conversation. Although this garden will take a decade for its unique character to emerge, it will become a favorite haunt for residents and visitors as it grows into its full majesty.

The garden is shaped in a spiral, a reference both to the spiraling kundalini energy of the dragon and to the shape these mythic creatures often assume in Asian art, their tails stretching out from their circled bodies. The garden's central tree is the unusual dragon's-eye pine, named for its long needles banded with red and green rings. Next to it are two tall, bluish columns of Chinese Dragon spruce with unusual purplish-gray bark. Spiraling beyond are three pyramidal Black Dragon Japanese cedars, whose bright green growing tips dot the dark older foliage.

Next come three evergreen Japanese holly of the variety called Black Dragon; these mounding shrubs bear dark green clustered leaves on intricately twisting branches. Three Scarlet Dragon azaleas grow to five feet tall, bearing masses of brilliant red flowers in mid-spring; their dense evergreen foliage provides privacy at the opening to the garden. Finally, two tiny Green Dragon Japanese holly form the dragon's tail.

Around this tree spiral, plant drifts of Marbled Dragon ivy, with its white-veined, multi-toned leaves, interspersed with Silver Dragon liriope, a magnificent variegated lily-turf groundcover whose spikes of lavender flowers brighten the path in late summer. Draw the groundcovers out at least two feet beyond the last holly bush, bringing the dragon's tail to as sharp a point as possible.

Once the plantings are in, pave the path with cedar chips or other natural material. A stone or paved path is inappropriate to the feeling of a forest glade that you are striving to create. As the pines and spruces mature, they add their litter to the pathways, creating a more natural ambiance.

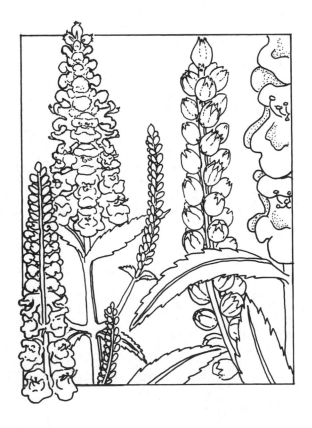

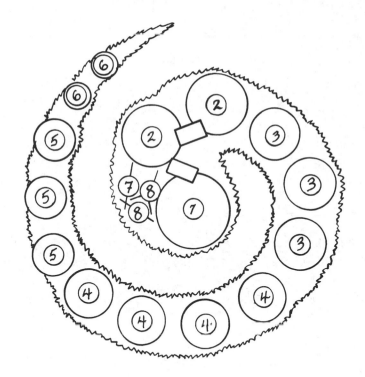

A Spiral of Trees

STRUCTURAL COMPONENTS

- cedar chips or other natural paving material
- bench or rustic chairs

PLANT LIST

1. Dragon's-eye Japanese red pine (*Pinus densiflora* 'Oculus-Draconis')
2. Chinese Dragon spruce (*Picea asperata*)
3. Black Dragon Japanese cedar (*Cryptomeria japonica Knaptonensis*)
4. Black Dragon Japanese holly (*Ilex crenata* 'Black Dragon')
5. 3 Scarlet Dragon azaleas (*Rhododendron Kurume Hybrid* 'Scarlet Dragon')
6. 2 Green Dragon Japanese holly (*Ilex crenata*)
7. 10 Marbled Dragon ivy (*Hedera helix* 'Marbled Dragon')
8. 20 Silver Dragon lilyturf (*Liriope spicata* 'Silver Dragon', shown on page 151)

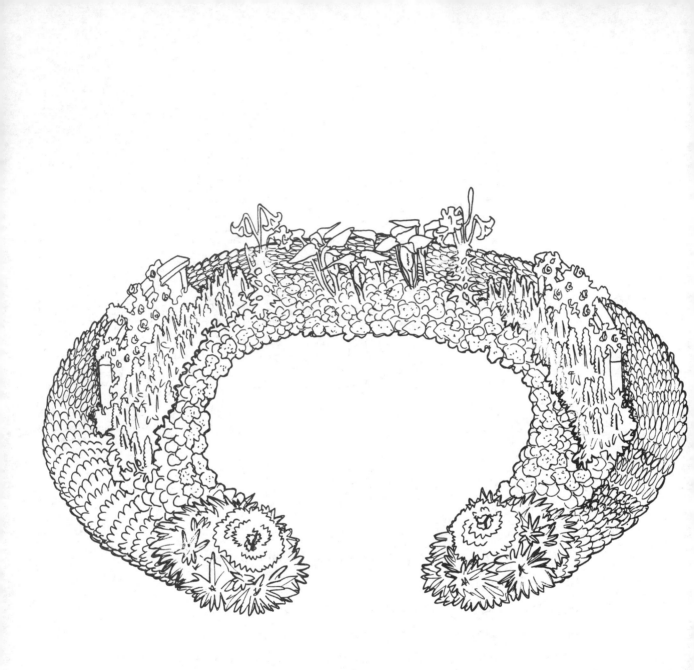

Design II: A Two-Headed Dragon Flower Garden

The second garden takes its shape from a classic form of Viking jewelry: a bracelet or neckpiece whose ends each have a dragon's head. This is said to represent the amphisbaena, the two-headed dragon of European legend. Like the Viking artifact, the garden is circular, with an opening between the two dragon's heads. Entering the small space in the garden's center demands that one walk between the heads, which symbolically calls to mind the role of dragons as guardians between worlds. Guarded by this dragon, the center of your garden is a precious space indeed.

Comprising the scaly backs of the dragon are two trellises planted with roses of the variety called Magic Dragon, a disease-resistant, vigorous plant that covers itself throughout the season with dark red pompoms like dragon's scales. Manufactured trellises are quite workable in this garden plan if laid sideways rather than upright. Should you be inspired to build one, a trellis with a gracefully scalloped top would even more vividly capture the serpentine sense of the dragon's form.

Only relatively few plants are used in this garden, but they are used in abundance. As they are perennials, you may wish to build this garden gradually, dividing and propagating the plants annually. It is possible, of course, to create the garden in one year with sufficient plants. When completed, the garden will be an undulating mass of pink and reddish blooms shining like dragon's scales among the green leaves—and plants whose names recall the beings you are honoring.

The dragon's eyes are formed by two of the dwarf Japanese holly called Green Dragon. With its deep green, rounded leaves, this slow-growing evergreen plant winks at you, even in winter when the remainder of the dragon is sleeping. Around these holly bushes, plant the variegated ground-covering lilyturf called Silver Dragon. This rapidly spreading grassy perennial forms a soft hair that offsets the dragon's eyes.

A band of the beloved perennial creeper Dragon's Blood sedum forms the belly of this dragon. Glossy, with cascades of reddish flowers throughout the season, this hardy plant also spreads quickly. Behind it and before the trellises, establish several drifts of false dragonhead, whose pink flowers echo, in miniature, the dragons' heads of the garden's entry. Growing to two feet tall, these long-time garden favorites spread quickly and make excellent cut flowers.

Between the two rose trellises, you may plant several glorious but expensive Black Dragon lilies, a garden favorite for more than three decades for its exceptionally tall, fragrant white trumpet with deep maroon exterior. Its extreme height (five to eight feet) requires staking. At the lilies' feet (or in place of them), plant a drift of the spiky, purple-leaved Red Dragon fleeceflower, with long-lasting, white baby's-breath-like flowers.

Finally, on the outer edge of the garden, plant the spurge called Jade Dragon, a compact green-flowered plant whose scaly appearance recalls that of the mythic beast it is named after. A relatively short plant, it spreads to form leafy drifts to counterpoint the garden's bright red and pink blooms.

Should you wish to adapt this garden for conversation or meditation, a bench can be set between the two trellises. You may add porcelain flowerpots with dragon designs at the sides of the bench to reinforce the garden's theme.

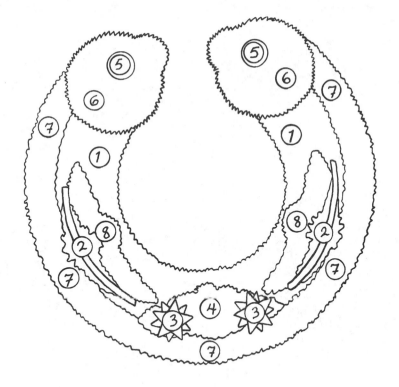

A Two-Headed Dragon Flower Garden

PLANT LIST

1. 8 Dragon's Blood sedum (*Sedum spurium* 'Dragon's Blood')

2. 2 Magic Dragon roses (*Rosa* 'Magic Dragon')

3. 2 Black Dragon lilies (*Lilium* 'Black Dragon')

4. 6 Red Dragon fleeceflowers (*Persicaria microcephala* 'Red Dragon')

5. 2 Green Dragon Japanese holly (*Ilex crenata* 'Green Dragon')

6. 10 Silver Dragon lilyturfs (*Liriope spicata* 'Silver Dragon')

7. 20 Jade Dragon spurges (*Euphorbia mellifera* 'Jade Dragon')

8. 20 false dragonheads (*Physostegia Virginiana*, shown on page 154)

Optional: Black Dragon lily (*Lilium leucanthum* 'Black Dragon')

A Fairy Garden

When a land is crushed by war, its divinities often are transformed into frightening monsters by the victorious invaders. Greek mothers warned their children about Lamia, the bogey-woman who would eat them alive. Semitic peoples feared the succubus Lilith, who would seduce and then devour them. Irish storytellers wove tales of the cannibal woman of the mountains, whose name changed according to the region. Yet Lamia, Lilith, and the mountain hag were originally powerful goddesses of the indigenous folk. When they lost their cosmic power, these goddesses lived on in the nightmares and folktales of those who conquered them.

But some divinities were too beloved to be demonized. They were disempowered in a different way: they were shrunk, dwarfed, or otherwise diminished by those who hoped that their power would also be lessened. The fairies and elves of various sorts that appear in so many mythologies were often originally greater gods. They remained with their people in miniature form, continuing to care for them and to answer their prayers.

Among the Celts of Ireland, Brittany, Scotland, Wales, Cornwall, and the Isle of Man, the fairy world was an especially important storage area for divinities that were forcibly abandoned with the coming of Christianity, according to the great scholar W. Y. Evans-Wentz. To the Celtic peoples, among whom the fairy faith remains strong, fairyland is not a separate world but rather an altered state of consciousness. The fairies inhabit our world but are normally invisible to us. They live in lakes and bogs, dancing magically and singing their sweet songs. They are especially in control of fertility: of people, of cattle, of the land itself. They are best honored by setting out a bit of food, especially milk, each evening.

Sometimes, the tales say, fairies appear in our mundane world, but this is not usually good news to humans. They may steal a lovely infant, replacing it with one of their own wizened little things. Or they may seduce an attractive man or woman, holding the beloved until they tire of the passion. But the rejected one can never thereafter find human love sufficiently enchanting and pines away unto death for love of fairyland. Only very few, like the great bard Thomas the Rhymer or the musician O'Carolan, come back to tell us of the beauties of fairyland and of the fairies themselves.

In creating a garden dedicated to the fairies, we invoke great powers—powers not to be trifled with. In Ireland, source of much fairy lore, no one would deliberately invite fairies into their garden, for these "good neighbors" are recognized as being more powerful than humans. This garden is designed to honor the fairy folk, not to attract them. According to Irish tradition, it would be foolhardy to purposely draw them near. If they want to visit you, they will—but don't expect you can control their actions if they do!

A Garden in Pots for Patio, Roof, Porch, or Deck

Not everyone has access to sufficient space to create a dancing lawn or unicorn meadow. But everyone has a bright corner that can be dedicated to the fairies and decked with pots of plants named in honor of them; thus, this Fairy Garden is adaptable to many locations. And, because the plants are grown in pots, this garden can be readily altered to fit your specific location requirements—arranged to climb up front steps, lengthened to fit a narrow balcony, even clumped under lights for an indoor extravaganza of bloom. You could even decide to re-create this garden in a corner of the garden rather than in pots, for these hardy perennials should thrive in zones 4–8.

Most plants named for fairies are, not surprisingly, miniatures, given the general assumption that they are a race smaller than human size. Thus your garden will have a diminutive, dainty quality. The plants selected for this garden are in soft pinks and pale whites, with delicate foliage and flowers. Because the largest plant will reach only three feet tall, you may wish to elevate some of the back plants to gain more vertical dimension. A large terra-cotta pot, overturned, will provide sufficient support.

This plan suggests a low bench on one side of the patio. This is not intended as a seat for humans but as a diminutive place for the fairies to sit if they should visit, rather than intruding on the more human parts of the garden. Seated there, they will be surrounded by a mass of long-blooming, lightly fragrant flowers and be satisfied to stay in their own space.

Because of the flexibility of pot gardens, you can rearrange this garden continually through the summer to best display the collection of blooms. Most of these flowers are excellent for cutting, so you'll be able to construct indoor arrangements of these compatible miniatures with ease. Because these plants are perennials, be certain to give them ample food throughout their growing season, as the limited soil in their pots will not provide sufficient nourishment. In winter, store them in an unheated garage, a cold frame, or the basement, for pots provide substantially less protection from the elements than the earth itself. Keep them barely moist, never wet, so that they neither dry out entirely nor rot. Some plants may flourish throughout the winter inside the house, but most require a period of dormancy and darkness.

The garden's theme is one of those that may tempt the gardener into kitsch: little fairy ornaments, fairies painted on the flowerpots, and suchlike. Better design will be achieved by offsetting the delicacy of the plants in this garden with strong, simple pot forms. You may wish to add color to this basically pink garden with one or more deep green, white, or even maroon glazed pots, although plain terra cotta will do well too.

Two rather large flowering shrubs form the foundation of this garden. Each demands a pot at least twelve inches in diameter. One is the famous antique miniature called The Fairy, a heritage rose whose arching canes carry masses of tender pink, ruffled flowers for many months. The bush, which should not be pruned, will grow quite large, perhaps three feet or more. Its canes are strong enough to thrive without a trellis, but you may use one to support its flourishing growth.

The other pot will be home to the Fairy's Dust clematis, whose dainty lavender-pink flowers make it an excellent choice to combine with The Fairy. Clematis requires a trellis, which should be planted firmly in the pot before you plant the vine. When you move the pot, beware of knocking the trellis over and tearing the vine. Although its ultimate size is somewhat smaller than the rose across from it, this clematis will reach nearly three feet within a few years.

A smaller variation of The Fairy joins it on the patio: Lovely Fairy, a spot of deeper pink, which has the famous attributes of heavy blooming and ease of growth of its ancestor. Although not heavily fragrant, these miniature roses make up for that lack with their casual exuberance and hardiness.

Next, place Pink Fairy baby's breath where it will add its delicate pastel pink flowers in clouds throughout the summer. Nearby, add pots of Sprite dwarf astilbe, with dark, ferny foliage and airy, abundant pink flowers. Two pots of the peach-pink daylily called Fairy Tale accentuate the pale pinks in this collection, as does the deep pink of the miniature rose Fairy Moss, whose semidouble blooms are continual throughout the season.

Should you desire a hanging basket to fill in the air space above this garden, you can plant Fairy Bells, an arch-stemmed vine whose white flowerbells will be among the first to bloom in this garden each summer. Be certain to keep this plant moist and cool.

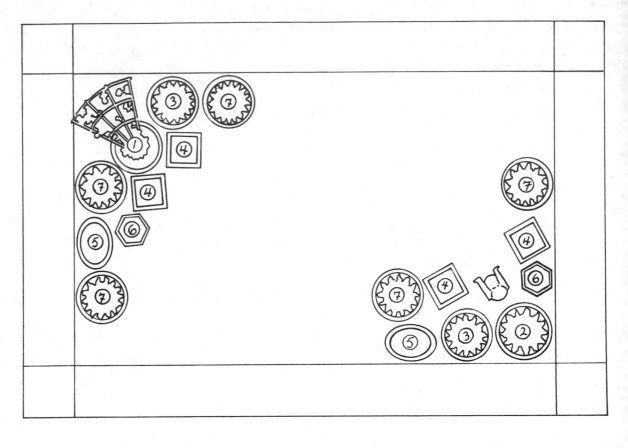

A Fairy Garden

STRUCTURAL COMPONENTS

- a small bench or chair
- variety of pots
- trellis (for the clematis)

PLANT LIST

1. 1 Fairy Dust clematis (*Clematis* 'Fairy Dust')
2. 1 The Fairy rose (*Rosa* 'The Fairy')
3. 2 Lovely Fairy miniature roses (*Rosa* 'Lovely Fairy')
4. 4 Sprite dwarf astilbes (*Astilbe simplicifolia* 'Sprite')
5. 2 Pink Fairy baby's breath (*Gypsophila paniculata* 'Pink Fairy')
6. 2 Fairy Tale daylilies (*Hemerocallis* 'Fairy Tale')
7. 5 Fairy Moss miniature roses (*Rosa* 'Fairy Moss')

Optional: Fairy Bells (*Disporum hookeri*)

Kuan-Yin's Garden of Mercy

Once, in China, there lived a little girl named Miao Shan. From her earliest days, she meditated so constantly on the Divine that she at last decided to become a nun and spend her life in prayer. But her ambitious father did not understand that his daughter was a prodigy of holiness. He demanded that she marry a wealthy man so that when the father was old, the husband would keep him comfortable.

When Miao Shan refused to marry, her father had her sent into the forest with soldiers, who were instructed to kill her. Before they could do so, a tiger snatched the young woman from them—but it did not eat her. Instead, it sent her on a journey into the world between the worlds, where she saw souls in torment, having died without fulfilling their lives' missions. Full of compassion, the young woman went back to earth even more determined to live in holiness.

And so she did, meditating and praying every moment until she had attained such enlightenment that she was ready to be transfigured into a Buddha. At the very last moment before she would have reached nirvana, however, she paused. Remembering all those who still suffer, whether in this life or beyond it, she turned back to aid them.

And thus the little girl Miao Shan became the great Kuan-Yin, called "she who hears the weeping world." She became one of the most popular figures in Chinese religion and traveled as well to nearby Japan, where she was known as Kwannon.

This Chinese bodhisattva (one who is almost a Buddha) deserves a corner of your garden, for we all have cares and concerns from which we need respite. This garden was inspired by the traditional Chinese scholar's garden, whose purpose was to assist the viewer in connecting to nature's spiritual force. Such a garden creates a peaceful spot for meditation and contemplation, a place where you may imagine Kuan-Yin relieving your cares. Once established, it requires very little care. You can rest there without hearing the demanding call of garden work. Similarly, it is designed to demand little artificial irrigation.

Because Kuan-Yin is honored in Japan as well as China, this garden employs some stylistic features of the Zen garden, especially in the placement of rocks representing a stone river; some plants associated with Japanese gardens are also used. Simplicity, important to both styles of garden, is gained through use of only a few plants in large drifts, as well as by the graceful curves of the borders. Rather than a profusion of bloom all at one time, the garden has a series of floral focal points that change with each season. In keeping with the gentleness of the bodhisattva, the color scheme is soft: pale pinks and yellows for the blooms, and a variety of textured greens in the trees and shrubs.

While designed to fit along a fence or boundary line, this garden can be adapted into a peninsula or island planting.

Establishing the Planting

This garden requires a length of approximately twenty-five feet along a fence or other boundary. Establish the front of the border by arranging a lawn hose or other flexible material until you find a pleasing curve that incorporates a small peninsula where the shrine will be placed. Double-dig the soil within the border: dig down twice the depth of one spade, moving the soil off to one side, then mix the soil with compost before replacing it in the garden. Enriching the soil this way will provide a good basis for the trees and perennials that will give you pleasure for years.

If you have sufficient room for a tall tree, anchor the planting with the magnificent Chinese pine (*Pinus tabulaeformis*), a tree that represents dignity and longevity in the symbol system of the Chinese garden. If you prefer to keep the plantings shorter, substitute the Japanese maple called Takinogawa ("waterfall river"), which will attain a fifteen-foot height. It has vibrant and complex fall colors of soft yellow and mauve, as well as a comforting mounded shape.

At the far end of the border, plant a lovely, small cascading Japanese maple, whose willowlike branches remind the viewer of Kuan-Yin's promise to relieve all the world's tears. Somewhat shorter (up to twelve feet) than the tree at the other end of the border, this maple helps set up a dynamic triangle in the planting area.

Between the two trees, leave an opening of some ten feet, then plant a staggered row of willows: the shorter (three-foot) Sekka fan-tail willow toward the garden's center, the taller (six-foot) Japanese pussy willow as you move toward the edge. The first draws the eye with its unusual twisted branches, while the second is covered in spring with huge silver catkins and in summer with grayish foliage.

Two-thirds of the way between the two anchoring trees, place the Kuan-Yin shrine. This portion of the planting will be most successful if you elevate it slightly above the rest of the garden. Before beginning to plant this area, build a mound of

topsoil approximately two feet high that slopes downward to the rest of the garden; it should be approximately eight feet in diameter. This will create the sense of a small private mountain that will be planted with dwarf trees and shrubs. Should you be unable to build a miniature mountain, arrange the trees and shrubs so that they screen the shrine from direct view and create a private zone of meditation.

Before building the shrine itself, create the seating area. At the bottom of your little hill, level the soil and pack it solidly. Then establish a kidney-shaped irregular pavement of small polished river stones. Create a path from the edge of the border to this site, using the river stones. If you do not mind sitting on the ground, this is all you need to do. If you prefer having an elevated seat, find a simple, unornamented stone bench or a perforated Chinese porcelain stool for the spot.

Near the summit of your small peak, create a level area approximately one foot in diameter and pave it, like the seating area, with river stones. Set a statue of Kuan-

Yin upon this pavement. Chinese gift stores sell many varieties, one of the most pleasing of which is the simple white porcelain variety showing Kuan-Yin gracefully offering her hand in mercy to the devotee. Although the shrine will be protected by its plantings, you may wish to remove porcelain objects during harsh weather, or you may use a cement outdoor statue.

Behind the shrine, on the far side of your miniature mountain, plant one of the most important plants in the Chinese garden: the flowering plum that represents renewal, for as one of the earliest of all flowering shrubs, it reminds us each spring of rebirth. There are many cultivars of plum available, including *Prunus blireiana*, with its softly pink double blossoms, and *Prunus maritima*, the fragrant beach plum. As you gaze upon this splendid small tree in early spring, feel the peace the ever-renewing seasons can bring.

Farther down the slope, place a specimen of the lovely little dwarf maple called Oto Hime for the Japanese goddess of the ocean, a mythic figure who resembles Kuan-Yin in her sea-borne form. A genetic dwarf that needs no pruning, this tree only grows to two feet tall but spreads widely and, like other maples, offers stunning fall color. Its complex and densely branched form provides winter interest as well.

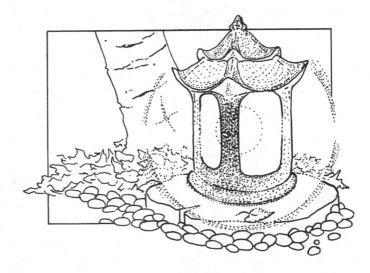

Down the slopes of the mountain, plant chrysanthemums, another important symbol in Chinese gardens, representing courage; this familiar fall flower is also important in Japan, where it symbolizes royalty. Among the innumerable cultivars of chrysanthemum available, the soft yellow Peace is especially appropriate to recall Kuan-Yin's merciful energies as well as to reflect the overall color scheme of this garden. Between the bamboo and the border's edge, plant masses of the small, hardy daylily named for Kuan-Yin. Its clear, pale pink blooms are long lasting even in drought and provide late summer color.

Between the slope and the weeping maple, plant several specimens of the tree peony Tracery of White Jade. In China, the peony is symbolic of the gentle strength of the feminine principle, as well as indicating wealth in the symbology of the Chinese garden. This plant's snowy, fringed flowers will appear not long after the plum has ceased to bloom. Beneath them, and extending across the border to its farther end, mass the small bamboo called Dwarf Whitestripe (*Pleioblastus fortunei*), with its bold white borders. Bamboo appears in every Chinese garden, symbolizing strength because of its tenacious habit of growth. In this garden, it reminds us of the gentle perseverance of Kuan-Yin's mercy.

As a final touch, place a stone lantern beneath the taller of the garden's anchor trees. Designed to be especially beautiful when covered with snow, these lanterns are used in Japanese tea gardens as evening illumination. A candle burning within the stone lantern casts a flickering, unforgettable light that can serve as a reminder of Kuan-Yin's ever-present mercy. Surround this lantern with the Kuan-Yin daylily to distinguish it further.

Kuan-Yin's Garden of Mercy

STRUCTURAL COMPONENTS

- small polished river stones
- statue of Kuan-Yin
- stone/concrete bench or porcelain stool
- stone lantern

PLANT LIST

1. 1 Chinese pine (*Pinus tabulaeformis*) or Japanese maple (*Acer japonicum*) Takinogawa ('Waterfall River')

2. 1 cascading Japanese maple (*Acer palmatum* 'Omurayama')

3. 5 Sekka Japanese fan-tail willows (*Salix udensis* 'Sekka')

4. 5 Japanese pussy willows (*Salix chaenomeloides*)

5. 1 flowering plum (*Prunus blireiana* or *Prunus maritime*)

6. 1 Oto Hime dwarf maple (*Acer palmatum* 'Oto hime')

7. 10 chrysanthemums

8. 7 Kuan-Yin daylilies (*Hemerocallis* 'Kuan Yin')

9. 3 Tracery of White Jade peonies (*Paeonia* 'Tama Sudare')

10. 10 Dwarf Whitestripe bamboos (*Pleioblastus fortunei*)

Two Sun Gardens

Since the Renaissance, Western science has placed the sun at the center of our planetary system. For millennia before that, the sun was central to the religion and mythology of virtually all people the world over.

And why not? Life without the sun is unimaginable. The sun provides us more than delightful warmth and brilliant golden light. Plants literally digest the sun's light, creating food through photosynthesis. We, in turn, eat the plants directly or, via animals, indirectly. Thus the sun can be said to feed us as well as keep us warm. In addition, our own bodies require sunlight for optimal functioning, as those who suffer from Seasonal Affective Disorder (SAD) can attest.

The sun has often been personified in male form. The Greek archer and poet god Apollo is perhaps best known today. The Muses were his servants, for art needs both physical light to be seen and the light of inspiration to be created. Apollo ruled divination and prophecy as well, for the sun sees all.

But in addition to such sun gods, there are innumerable sun goddesses. Saule of Lithuania and Latvia drove her brown horses through the sky each day, stopping to shear the forests with golden scissors so that the trees could never block her light. Sunnu of the Scandinavians ran through the sky trying to escape the pursuing Fenris wolf, who would one day eat her alive—but not before she gave birth to her daughter sun, who thereafter will ride her mother's roads each day.

In Native America, the Cherokee honored the sun as the goddess Unelanahi, "the apportioner," for she divided out the hours as she crossed the sky. She was the inventor of the strawberry, which she created in order to draw men and women together in sensual pleasure. In Japan, the sun goddess Amaterasu-omi-Kami once plunged the earth into darkness by hiding in a dark rock cave. Only the creation of a magical mirror drew her forth—that and the bawdy jokes told by Uzume, the shaman goddess.

To these and to all other divinities of the sun, it is most appropriate to build a garden. For the sun is one of the gardener's closest allies, the others being the rain and groundwater that plants drink, and the soil in which they flourish. Even from behind clouds, even in winter's chill, the sun sends forth its vital light. These two gardens send back a living prayer of thanks.

Positioning the Solar Garden

Two variations on the same theme—a small sun pattern created of plants with solar names—are offered here. Most solar-named plants are, it should come as no surprise, yellow-leaved or yellow-flowering. It should also come as no surprise that these plants require significant sun to thrive. Thus the best placement for either of these gardens is as an island in the center of a lawn. The green carpet surrounding them emphasizes the garden's shape and color.

Be certain to place the garden where you can see it from a window or deck looking down upon it, so that you may best enjoy its shape. At eye level you will see the lovely golden colors of the plants and flowers, but to appreciate the full pattern you'll need an elevation above the plantings.

Design I: A Daylily Extravaganza

The first variation of this circular garden represents a freeform sun with twisting, fiery waves of color emanating from it. It is a somewhat more difficult garden to plant than the simple second variation, but its charming combination of yellow daylilies and other yellow-flowered plants set against a dark border make it worth the additional labor.

The sunniest area of many yards is already covered with turf, so your first step may be to remove the turf to permit planting. To construct the garden, you'll first have to establish the freeform perimeter. To do this, use dark river pebbles (available at most nurseries) to "draw" the outline of the sun's burning disc directly where the garden will be. First, drive short posts at the base and points of each ray's triangle; connect them with twine to establish the overall outline of the sun. Then, within each "ray," build a twisting line of pebbles, after which you can remove the stakes and twine. The pattern given here is merely a guide. Your own garden shape will be organically formed there in your own garden. You need not worry about making mistakes, for the pebbles are easily moved to correct any awkward lines that may emerge. Before planting, make certain that you are satisfied with the sun's "rays" by viewing the design for several days at various times of day. Once you are satisfied with the design, expand each ray's border to approximately three inches by installing more stones on the outer side of the original boundary stones.

The dominant flower in this small patch is the daylily, which gracefully bends over the perimeter pebbles even in early spring. But at the center are several taller plants that form the sun's "body." In spring, the warm, raspberry-tinged, semidouble flowers of the Helios tree peony, named for an ancient Greek sun god, illuminate the garden. Later seasons see its dark leaves forming a centerpiece to the garden design. In midsummer, the brilliant yellow Sundrenched lily will flourish and provide another punctuation of solar color.

The daylilies offer a choice. You may select one variety and plant the entire garden with it, but a more exciting possibility is to mix the various daylilies to create a blooming tapestry of golds and yellows. Some varieties to choose from are Hyperion, named for yet another Greek sun god, a prolific and very fragrant soft yellow flower that naturalizes and spreads easily and, at forty inches tall, should be planted toward the center of the bed; Sun's Eye, a clear yellow, early blooming, large flower on thirty-two-inch stems; and Solar Crest, a shorter (twenty-inch) creamy yellow ruffled variety.

Interplant these daylilies with daffodils, which will bloom early and spend themselves before the daylilies are stirring. The daylily foliage hides the dying daffodil leaves as summer progresses. Sun Disc is an intensely fragrant small (eight- to twelve-inch) daffodil that, as its name suggests, has a flat, disclike shape.

A Daylily Extravaganza

STRUCTURAL COMPONENTS

- dark river pebbles

PLANT LIST

1. 3 Helios tree peonies (*Paeonia suffruticosa* 'Helios')

2. 3 Sundrenched lilies (*Lilium* 'Sundrenched')

3. Mixed daylilies: Hyperion (*Hemerocallis* 'Hyperion'), Sun's Eye (*Hemerocallis* 'Sun's Eye'), Solar Crest (*Hemerocallis* 'Solar Crest')

4. Sun Disc daffodils (*Narcissus jonquilla* 'Sun Disc')

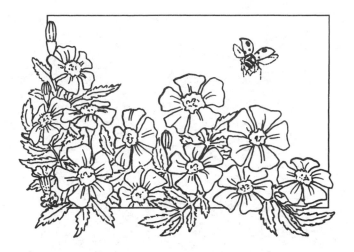

Design II: *Marigolds and Golden Hostas*

An easier garden to plant—but one that needs to be planted with annuals each spring—our second design variation is quite simple. A single large yellow hosta, surrounded by six smaller brilliant hostas, is in turn surrounded by triangles of upright marigolds. Easy and effective, this garden repays the needed annual replacement.

The central plant is the rare Solar Flare hosta, the largest-leaved of the golden hostas. As it matures, it grows almost as large as a shrub, although it dies back annually. Unlike most hostas, which prefer shade, this plant thrives in sun, which makes its pale yellow leaves more vividly bright. It grows into a stunning centerpiece for this garden.

Around the Solar Flare, plant a circle of Sundance, another hosta that performs well in sun. Smaller than its impressive relative Solar Flare, this hosta has dark green, golden-edged leaves that grow nearly two feet tall. Finally, circle the hosta with dwarf yellow (or golden, but not orange) marigolds, readily available in flats each spring. Then, being careful to make the rays symmetrical, plant groups of two or three, followed by ray "points" of a single marigold. These long-flowering lovelies shine on sunny days and cloudy ones alike through late fall.

Marigolds and Golden Hostas

PLANT LIST

1. 1 Solar Flare hosta (*Hosta* 'Solar Flare')
2. 6 Sundance hostas (*Hosta* 'Sundance')
3. 4–5 six-packs dwarf yellow marigolds (any variety)

A Sorcerer's Secret Garden

What is it about a walled garden that we find so magical? No matter what our age, we grow soft-eyed when we remember the secret gardens of literature and film and painting. Such a garden is a place of safety and retreat—a carefree, wistful place that beckons us all. We may never have had such a secret garden, but something in us yearns for one.

French philosopher Gaston Bachelard, the poet of space, contends that we all recognize an experience of "intimate immensity" in which our inner vastness finds reflection in such terrestrial features as the ocean or a mountain range. Its opposite, he tells us, is the primal pleasure of the nest. There our needs for security are met, and there, paradoxically, we can encounter our true wildness, our animal need for nurturance and care.

The walled garden is such a nest. There, in voluptuous privacy, we can feel secure enough to envision utter freedom. There we can feel safe enough to encounter the possibilities of life. There, in quiet stillness, we can hear our heart's words.

The ideal secret garden would be behind old stone walls, shrouded with ageless ivy. We would find it one day in an overlooked corner of the estate, spying its weathered door amid the tangled vines. Its single door would be opened by a skeleton key—found under a nearby rock—that fits into a rusted old lock. Inside, the walls would disappear behind plants that tumble over each other, long since untended. It would be a perfect image of wilderness in containment.

You may not have a vast estate with an overgrown secret garden already planted, but you can certainly find a corner where such a secret garden can be placed. You may not have century-old plantings, but you can create an abundantly overwrought look within a few gardening seasons by using fast-growing plants and by crowding annuals in among the perennials that, after several years, need no such support.

Although some might expect a sorcerer's garden to be filled with magical herbs for brewing potions, this one is for the dreaming self, the part of the magician that wants to sit awhile and let the deep self speak. This garden is made more mysterious and evocative by the use of dark-blooming plants. It is intended as a secret retreat for the urban sorcerer, a place open only to the sky, a place for private dreaming and enchantment. You may wish to work magic there or you may wish to simply let this garden's magic work on you.

Positioning the Garden

Even a small property has room for this garden, which requires space of perhaps fifteen feet for each side. Ideally it would be placed somewhere it can be discovered anew each time it is entered. One could certainly erect four walls smack in the middle of a lawn, but where would be the secrecy? No, look for a place where a pocket of space exists already, like at the rear of or beside a garage, or in a shady corner at the edge of the lot. Be certain to select a place where there is some sun during the day. If you have a place in deep shade, limit your plantings to the hosta and other shade-lovers mentioned below.

This garden is best placed where at least one "wall" already exists as building or fence. You may even find a place where three walls already exist—a corner where a tall fence's corner abuts a building, for instance. Be aware of the aerial view in placing your garden. A space between two buildings might be perfect in other ways, but a neighbor's window directly above your secret garden eliminates the privacy this garden needs.

When you have located your space, begin by building the remaining walls. The most romantic secret gardens have brick walls, but only go to that trouble if you already have established brickwork. Otherwise, erect sections of fence at least six feet high that match what exists or that are in keeping with the surroundings. The walls are intended to be covered with quick-growing plants, so stability and strength is more important than appearance. You might build the additional walls yourself, using prefabricated fence panels. Take care to properly position and install the fence posts, for a fence that tilts within a few years won't add charm. Hiring a fence builder should not be an especially expensive proposition for a small secret garden and ensures a solid foundation for your plantings.

Within one of your added walls, position the garden's doorway. Do not place it directly in the center of the wall, but rather offset it to one side for mysterious asymmetry. If you find it makes the garden more secret to stoop upon entering it, have the door cut to four or four and a half feet tall. Otherwise, make the gate a conventional six feet tall for ease of entry.

Before you begin planting, place a spiral of flagstones that comprise the garden path. If the floor of your garden is not level, use that to your advantage by having the flagstones follow natural curves. Be certain, however, to position the flagstones firmly (and flatly) so that you and your visitors do not stumble.

If you have moss nearby, gather some and place it in a blender with some unflavored yogurt (make certain it has active yogurt cultures) and a quart of water. Liquefy and paint over your flagstones. The moss quickly spreads and your flagstone path looks suitably ancient and romantic.

Finally, place a bench near the end of the flagstone spiral. To match the dark-toned plants and flowers in this secret garden, paint the bench dark forest green. A dark wooden or metal bench also blends in well. You are now ready to fill the garden with plants, shrubs, and vines to create a mysterious retreat.

Planting the Secret Garden

Begin with the walls. Within a few years they will be virtually hidden with the vines you'll plant. This garden, more than others, takes some time to develop, so be patient and enjoy your garden as it cloaks itself in greenery. Any number of vines are appropriate to shroud your gardens' walls, depending on your gardening zone. Ivies are generally adaptable and grow strongly. Ornamental kiwi, which does not produce fruit, is another option. You may wish to mix several vines for leaf variety.

Once the vines are in place, you're ready to plant the remaining perennials, shrubs, and self-sowing annuals. Note that the garden is designed with one corner planted with perennials that demand the most sun. Feel free to alter the location of gates and the direction of the path, but make sure to keep the plants' demands for sun uppermost in your planning and planting.

Inside the gate, plant the shade-loving hosta Edge of Night on either side of the path. As they grow, these impressive giants create a suitable jungle to greet visitors. Beside these, place drifts of the annual coleus Wizard, and be sure to nip off flower stalks as they form for best appearance. Along the right-hand wall, plant a collection of iris, mixing the deep purple Dark Passion and the black/dark maroon Superstition. To the left of the path, plant drifts of the unusual geranium Black Diamond, with its pale flowers blotched with black.

At the first corner, and in the corner opposite as well, plant mountain witch-alder (pictured below), a short shrub whose early, brushy blooms perfume the

garden. Beneath its open branches, plant the small pansy Black Devil, whose dark faces shine out of their mounds of foliage. Start these annuals in flats indoors, then move out when weather permits. Tuck three or five (never an even number) of these darlings in wherever the perennials have not yet filled a space.

As you move toward the sunniest corner, plant two drifts of sun-loving daylilies, mixing Court Magician (purple touched with white), Cast a Spell (also purple and white), and Purple Magic (purple with yellow). In the sunny corner, plant one or two of the shrub rose Alchymist, whose billowy, multicolored blooms seem to be turning into gold.

A huge drift of the unusual rudbeckia Green Wizard greets the eye as you turn on the spiraling path. This green-petaled, dark-centered flower grows to four feet tall, and its dark cones last long into winter outdoors and make good dried arrangements indoors. Beneath it, place a smaller drift of geranium. Beneath the bench, seed the delightful nemophila Total Eclipse. Although an annual, this plant self-seeds reliably so that you can continually enjoy its tiny, white-edged black flowers. It's a low-growing plant that should be encouraged to seed under the nearby taller perennials as well.

In the roughly circular center of the garden, where the path's spiral ends, put a moon-shaped curve of Blue Seer hosta, a puckered, deep-blue variety. Within the moon, plant a curved drift of alchemilla, the plant used by medieval alchemists to capture dew drops for their preparations. This plant forms attractive mounds with frothy, long-lasting, yellow-green blossoms. Finally, plant one specimen of the little black-berried holly called Inkberry, which grows slowly to nearly four feet but stays compact and lustrous.

Throughout the garden, tuck several varieties of tulip for spring bloom: the tall Queen of Night with its velvety maroon blooms; Black Swan, a more purplish maroon; and the late Black Pearl. In addition, you can encourage some smaller self-sowing annuals to spread throughout the spaces between the flagstones: the nemophilia mentioned above and the Bowles Black viola, a quick-spreading (some would say invasive) perennial with dark black faces and little yellow eyes.

As your sorcerer's garden ages, the plants fill out to form a romantic jungle of growth. This garden repays your planting with many dreamy, meditative hours.

A Sorcerer's Secret Garden

STRUCTURAL COMPONENTS

- sections of fence sufficient to enclose area

- gate or door

- approximately 20 large flagstones

- small darkly painted bench

1. Vines (select several): Ivies (*Hedera*); ornamental kiwi (*Actinidia kolomikta*)

2. 2 Edge of Night hostas (*Hosta* 'Edge of Night')

3. 12 Wizard coleus (*Solenostemon scutellariodes* 'Wizard')

4. 10 Black Diamond geraniums (*Geranium* 'Black Diamond')

5. 20 mixed irises: Dark Passion (*Iris germanica* 'Dark Passion'), Superstition (*Iris germanica* 'Superstition')

6. 2 mountain witch-alders (*Fothergilla major*)

7. 12–30 Black Devil pansies (*Viola* 'Black Devil')

8. 12 daylilies: Court Magician (*Hemerocallis* 'Court Magician'); Purple Magic (*Hemerocallis* 'Purple Magic'); Cast a Spell (*Hemerocallis* 'Cast a Spell')

9. 1 Alchymist shrub rose (*Rosa* 'Alchymist')

10. 10 Green Wizard rudbeckia (*Rudbeckia occidentalis* 'Green Wizard')

11. 20 Total Eclipse nemophila (*Nemophila menziesii*)

12. 2 Blue Seer hostas (*Hosta* 'Blue Seer')

13. 3 alchemillas (*Alchemilla mollis*)

14. 1 Inkberry holly (*Ilex glabra nigra*)

For Spring Bloom: Tulips: Queen of Night (*Tulipa* 'Queen of Night'); Black Swan (*Tulipa* 'Black Swan')

For Pathways: Total Eclipse nemophila (*Nemophila menziesii*) and Bowles Black viola (*Viola tricolor*)

The Unicorn Meadow

Of all mythical beasts, only one is truly at home in the garden. Griffins, basilisks, werewolves, hydras—these fierce beings make their homes in swamps and forests, canyons and night-shrouded mountains. And who, indeed, would want to lure them forth from such haunts, carrying their terrifying powers of destruction and transformation with them?

But the unicorn—that is another story. Who would not wish such a gentle being to visit our gardens, bringing its grace and power to our doorstep?

The lore of the wild unicorn is widely known. Almost 1,500 years ago, European bestiaries began to describe the goatlike little animal with its single sharp white horn rising from its brow. Despite its tiny size, the unicorn was both swift and fierce. It could not be captured by any hunter, no matter how diligent. However, should a virgin sit down in the center of a meadow frequented by unicorns, one might approach her and lay its head in her lap. She could then stroke it until it fell asleep…whereupon the hunter could capture the unicorn and lead it immediately to the palace of the king.

This is the gentler version of the story. In some tellings, the unicorn is killed in bloody battle by soldiers who have hidden in the woods behind the alluring virgin. Why kill the lovely unicorn? For its magical horn, said to ward off even the strongest poisons. Rare was the medieval or Renaissance ruler who did not keep a twisted ivory horn close at hand. Some even had servants especially designated to stir every glass of claret and every pot of stew with the unicorn's horn. Many died nonetheless, although their deaths somehow did not disprove the potent magic of the horn. And many lived despite the strong likelihood that the "unicorn horn" was an artificially worked walrus tusk.

Poisoning being less popular today, this unicorn meadow is offered with the presumption that those who build it want to honor unicorns, not kill them. This garden provides a restful setting for whatever still-wild unicorns might ramble through your town and is, as well, a fitting location for meditations on the mystic meaning of this fierce yet tender beast of legend.

Planting the Meadow

The best places to see unicorns are, ironically, in some of the world's largest cities. In New York at the Metropolitan Museum of Art's Cloisters and in Paris at the cloister of Cluny, you can see this fabled beast (and the moment-by-moment sequence of its hunt) in enormous and colorful medieval tapestries. On this wall is the "water-conning" feat, when the unicorn purifies water by kneeling before a stream and placing his horn into it. Over there, the maiden sits beneath the tree, a unicorn gazing into her mirror, its feet trustingly in her lap. In the tapestries that illustrate the milder version of the story, we see the unicorn in captivity, resting quietly within its circular corral. In the tapestries that end in slaughter, we see the unicorn valiantly fighting a dozen hunters, goring hounds and kicking knights wildly, then gallantly meeting the raised spears of its doom.

This garden plan is based on the flowers that appear in these medieval masterpieces. Their woven detail is so precise that we can identify the plants flourishing in the tree-circled meadow where the unicorn roams and is captured. Still available to gardeners today, these plants create a charming tapestry-like effect when planted as instructed. The garden is designed without structures or sculptures. While it might be tempting to chain a unicorn statue to a shrub within this little space, the result would be saccharine. Better to honor the spirit of the unicorn with an entirely natural garden.

While this garden is designed as a small circular island in the midst of lawn, surrounded by a short fence representing the heart's purity (and which, note, has a little gateway for the unicorn's entrance), it could be adapted to fit whatever space you have available. Should you have sufficient land, you might wish to replicate the full tapestry setting by planting a circle of dwarf fruit trees (apples, plums, and pears appear in the tapestries) within which the flowering plants can be placed. Such a circle should be approximately fifty feet in diameter for the trees' comfort. Given such a large space, underplant the trees with a low-growing groundcover, such as Roman chamomile, sprinkled with the plants mentioned below.

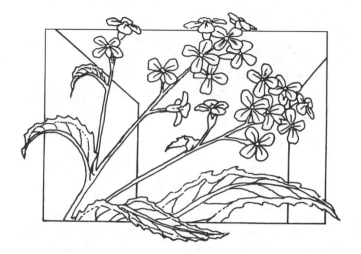

To establish the garden, select a sunny location. This small garden makes a fine island in the midst of lawn. Have a yard of good topsoil delivered, which you can form into a slight rise in the garden's center. If you are beginning with turf, use newspaper mulch to make the space useable quickly.

Space the plants out across the area, being careful to leave sufficient space between plants so that, even when fully grown, they do not touch each other. Approximately eighteen inches between plants should do nicely. Be sure to arrange the plants randomly, because regimented rows of plants destroy the illusion of a tapestry background. Similarly, do not group plants together, because the tapestries show the plants singly rather than in drifts.

The greatest temptation in planting this garden is to create a cottage-garden effect by massing plants too thickly. If you examine the tapestries, however, you can see that the plants are isolated, emphasizing the sculptural quality of their leaves and flowers. Enhance this effect and help keep down weeds by covering the soil between the plants with dark mulch.

Once the garden has been planted, install a short white fence around its perimeter, leaving open a space for the unicorn's entry. Preformed plastic fence sections are acceptable and are inexpensive. A handmade wooden fence might attract more unicorns, who are likely to be flattered by such attentions.

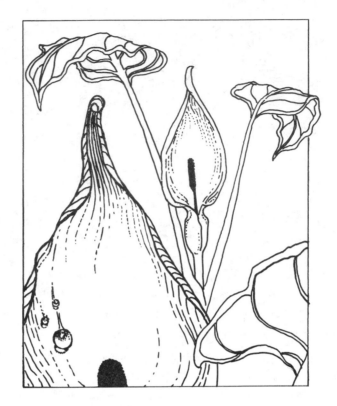

For this garden, only perennials have been used, although a few annuals—like the sweet-scented stock (*Matthiola*)—are visible in the tapestries. You may wish to include some stock in the first few years before your garden is well established and sufficiently full of bloom. Once the plants are established, however, another challenge presents itself: that of controlling invasive growth. Some of these perennials could outgrow their designated position if not controlled carefully, but dividing them annually provides you with additional plants for elsewhere in the yard—or for very thankful friends.

This garden's plants include sweet william, the cheery fragrant garden pink; searing red Maltese cross, called campion in the Middle Ages; the scallop-leaved healing herb called alchemilla, "little magical one," or lady's mantle; sculptural thistle; dainty lords and ladies (pictured above); daisy-flowered leopard's bane; fragrant phloxlike sweet rocket (pictured on page 197); friendly, familiar pansy-faced violets; and the much-loved pristine white Madonna lily. All are ancient plants with interesting histories, including use in herbal remedies.

Once established, this garden needs little care—but be careful not to disturb any unicorns you find sleeping there at dawn.

The Unicorn Meadow

Structural Components

- black weed-proofing woven material
- white picket-fence sections of wood or plastic

Plant List

1. 5 Maltese crosses (*Lychnis chalcedonica*)
2. 5 sweet williams (*Dianthus*)
3. 5 holy thistles (*Silybum marianum*)
4. 10 lady's mantles (*Alchemilla vulgaris*)
5. 6 leopard's banes (*Doronicum pardalianches*)
6. 5 lords and ladies (*Arum maculatum*)
7. 6 sweet rockets (*Hesperis matronalis*)
8. 10 mixed pansies (*Viola*)
9. 4 Madonna lilies (*Lillium candidum*)

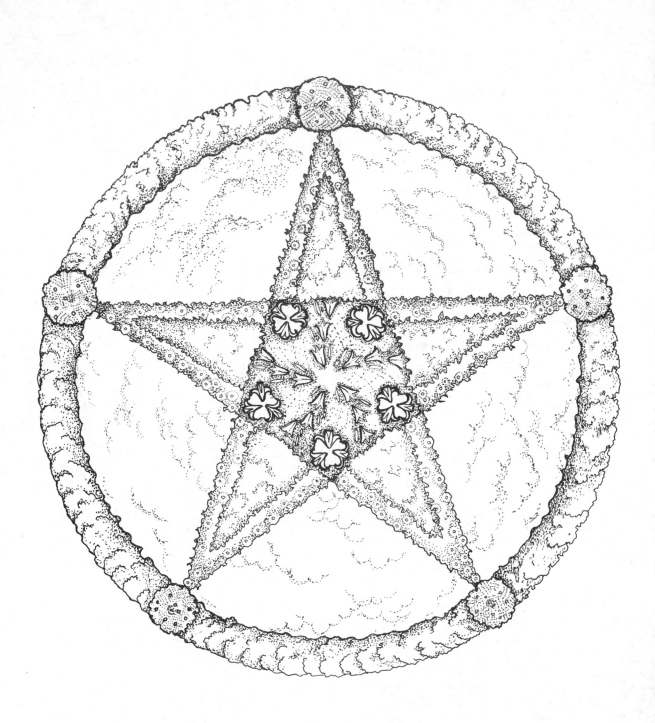

A Witch's Garden

In the old tales, witches always have gardens.

Remember Dame Gothel? She was the witch in "Rapunzel," the one whose walled garden was lush with magnificent flowers and herbs. From her window, Rapunzel's pregnant mother used to stare over the wall at that garden, which none dared enter for fear of its owner. One day the woman noticed a fine green patch of rampion, or spring ramps, a chivelike form of onion—*rapunzel*, in her language. A craving took hold of her. She could not sleep until she had some of that herb! And so her husband stole into the garden and stole the rampion. You know the rest of the story: the girl up the tower, the long golden hair, the prince. All this because of a woman's envy of the luxuriant growth of a witch's garden.

Or take Grimm's tale "Donkey Cabbages," wherein a young man eats a witch's cabbages and is turned into—you guessed it—a donkey. Or in "Briar Rose," the old witch—the "evil godmother" who curses the girl to whose christening she has not been invited—has the kind of control over rose bushes any gardeners would fancy, for they grow so high and strong that they encase the castle in which the girl sleeps.

If the witch is, as many have argued, a derogatory form of the wise woman, these witches of legend were reflections of the village midwife and herbalist. Imagine her little cottage almost smothered with the twining roses she loved and the herbs she needed for healing. Imagine how, when you opened the door, you'd be greeted with a sharp smell of stewing poultices and a vision of a cloud of herbs hanging over-head to dry. She would bustle up to you—don't you just see an energetic woman of indeterminate age, full of whim and vinegar?—and fix you with her astonishingly youthful eyes. Before you knew it, you'd have fallen under the spell of her learning and her wit, her passion for life and her concern for her community. After you left her presence, a tiny packet of mysterious medicine in your hand, life outside that cottage would seem a bit flat and stale. Is it any wonder that people thought they'd been bewitched?

Of course such a witch would have a garden. And of course it would become a thing of legend in her community. Witches need gardens like blacksmiths need anvils. The plants were the tools of her trade, her sources of nature's medicine. The willows gave her salicylic acid for headaches—natural aspirin. The raspberries, in addition to providing her sweets in the summer, gave her leaves to ease menstrual distress. There would be fennel for digestion, hops for sleep. Even the rose that twined about her little cottage—it produced ascorbic acid in its round, orange hips, a simple against scurvy and so much else.

Our witch knew the woodlands, too, for the wild medicines they produced. She knew all the best wild herb patches in the area and made annual treks to capture each of them for the year's potions. Perhaps she was the one who tamed some of them, like sprawling mint and sweet-scented chamomile. For this witch—these witches, thousands and thousands of such women—saw no absolute boundary between "wild" and "tame." She was intimate with all plants. Perhaps it was advancing age and arthritis that convinced her that, rather than walking to the next county for wild horehound to cure cough, she could transport twigs back and nurture them in a sunny spot.

For centuries such women served the rural communities of Europe. Then, tragically, society turned against them. Some scholars claim that at the birth of modern medicine, men in cities tried to destroy the village women whose old power threatened their newfound one. Others contend that these herbal healers bore the spores of old knowledge, perhaps even trained willing villagers in ancient rituals, and that the Inquisition targeted them as religiously unorthodox. Whatever the reason, untold numbers of healers lost their lives in the Burning Times. Like the savage burning of the Library of Alexandria, this holocaust destroyed knowledge at whose depth and breadth we can today only guess.

A Pentacle for a Witch's Garden

Any garden can be a witch's garden, so long as it is seeded with love and tended with concern. But why not plant one that especially honors those who lived (and died) as witches? This one is not the sprawling cottage yard of the medieval witch, rampant with necessary herbs. Such a garden cannot be planned or designed, for it emerges from long work with the cultivation of perennial herbs.

Rather, this is a modern witch's garden, a collection of perennial herbs mixed with flowers in the shape of what has become today's most recognizable symbol of witchcraft. The pentacle represents the five elements of earth, air, fire, water, and spirit. The circle around it contains these vital energies. This small garden can be used as part of a longer perennial border, be placed upon a hilly lawn, or form the centerpiece for a vegetable and herb garden.

The design is inspired by formal French potagers or kitchen gardens, in which flowers, herbs, and vegetables are combined in intricate patterns to delight eye as well as palate. Such gardens are typically composed of annual plants, but this combines a central planting of perennials that will shine for many years.

The Perennial Plantings

The five points of the central pentagon are marked by the aptly named magic lily. Late each summer, flower stalks jump from the bare ground, leap up to three feet in height, and open into fragrant trumpet lilies. The foliage follows, often lasting through the winter, then dies away before the next bloom comes. Delightful and surprising, these lilies make a bold statement in the central part of the design.

The remainder of the pentagon is filled with a variety of daylilies—or, if you prefer, one or two that especially suit your color preferences. Daylilies named for witches are remarkably common. Some to choose from are Merry Witch, rosy pink with a light chalky eye; Wicked Witch, dark maroon with ruffled edges; Witch's Thimble, cream with black-purple eye; and Purple Magic, medium purple with a bright yellow heart. You will find others as well among the thousands of daylilies available.

The arms of the starry pentacle are planted in a repeating combination of herbs: low-growing and fragrant chamomile forming a light-green border around darker-green mint. You can plant a different flavor mint in each arm to give yourself a choice between peppermint and spearmint and chocolate mint, to name just a few.

Finally, plant round clumps of Essex Witch dianthus—which open into fragrant mounds of fringed pink flowers—at each point of the star. This completes the perennial planting. To keep such a garden from losing its shape, you must regularly divide the perennials; every second year should suffice. (Or you can let the plants erode the design, slowly turning the pentacle into a rambling witch's cottage garden.)

The Annual Plantings

Only one of the two plants that comprise the remainder of the design is an annual. The other is a biennial but will be treated like an annual to provide consistent coverage in the design. These plants are sweet alyssum, the dainty low-growing white flower that forms the background to the pentacle, and parsley, which forms the green circle around the entire design. Both are readily (and relatively cheaply) available each spring from neighborhood garden shops. Growing your own seedlings will save money, but only attempt it if you have a strong light source and the patience to nurture the tiny seedlings and to properly harden them off.

Both plants have neat habits of growth, making them ideal to outline the pentacle vividly. When combined with the central perennial planting, these annuals provide definition rather than color to the overall design.

A Witch's Garden

1. 5 magic lilies (*Lycoris Squamigera*)

2. 10 daylilies, one variety or mixed: Merry Witch (*Hemerocallis* 'Merry Witch'); Wicked Witch (*Hemerocallis* 'Wicked Witch'); Witch's Thimble (*Hemerocallis* 'Witch's Thimble'); Purple Magic (*Hemerocallis* 'Purple Magic')

3. 15 mints, single variety or mixed (*Mentha*)

4. 35 chamomile, single variety or mixed (*Matricaria recutita/Matricaria chamomilla* or *Anthemis nobilis*)

5. 5 Essex Witch dianthus (*Dianthus* 'Essex Witch')

6. 50 sweet alyssum (*Lobularia maritima*)

7. 35 parsley (*Petroselinum crispum*)

Six

In Gaia's Name

Gaia

The wide blue sky wants to penetrate the earth.

The earth longs for utter union. See, it comes.

Rains fall as sky meets earth.

Rains fall. Earth bubbles with life.

Life springs forth from the damp soil:

flocks of sheep like clouds, oceans of wheat.

All gifts for earth's children. And one more:

peace. Peace that blossoms in a rain of love.

• • • • • •

Aeschylus, The Danaides

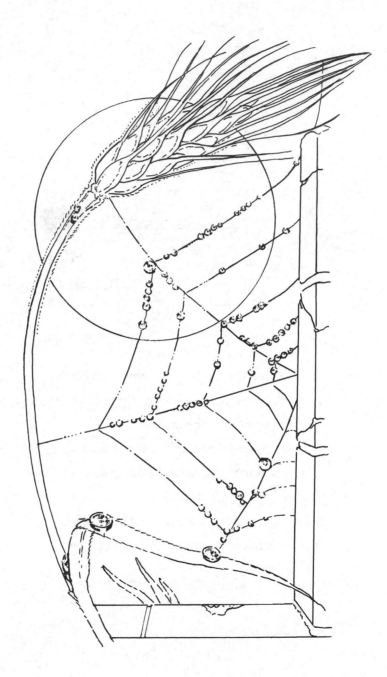

Once upon a time, the ancient Greeks said, there was no sun, no moon, and no stars. There was no water and no land. There was no air to breathe, no space beyond the atmospheres. There was nothing but formless chaos.

Light and dark, earth and sea and sky—all swirled together in a cosmic blur, a shapeless fog, a gray soup. Nothing was distinguished from anything else.

Yet this chaos was alive—not conscious yet, but alive—fecund, expanding, ceaselessly growing.

After untold ages, form emerged from primordial chaos. It was as though chaos had condensed into a sphere. And, unlike the chaos around her, this form had consciousness, for it had become the first of all divinities—deep-breasted Gaia, mother of us all.

She did not have the form of a human woman. Perhaps we cannot even call her a goddess, for she had no breasts except her mountains, no belly except her valleys, no blood except her running lava rivers. Gaia contained within her the male principle, to which she later gave birth, as well as the female. Later in this story the sexes would divide, but at this point Gaia was all.

This totality of being, this complete divinity, floated for unmeasured eons on the primal sea. Gaia, who observed the chaotic universe around her, watched as stars coalesced and suns began to glow in the dark sky, watched as the first meteors streaked across the faces of the first moons.

She was content within herself for more years than have been counted since humanity first walked upon the earth. For untold ages, Gaia was alone, so fascinated with the emergence of order from primal chaos that she was not for an instant lonely.

But slowly chaos receded, and the universe spun in its orderly way. Planets revolved around suns, and moons around planets. Light connected itself with heat and was no longer spread throughout the universe. Darkness separated itself, its black beauties now visible against the new light. Water formed, refining itself out of rock and soil.

Upon her own surfaces Gaia saw the changes. The lava rivers cooled, and fresh water flowed upon the earth's surfaces. The oceans withdrew into their basins, and mountains thrust themselves up over the plains. Clouds formed, white dancers in a sunlit sky. And Gaia saw that it was good.

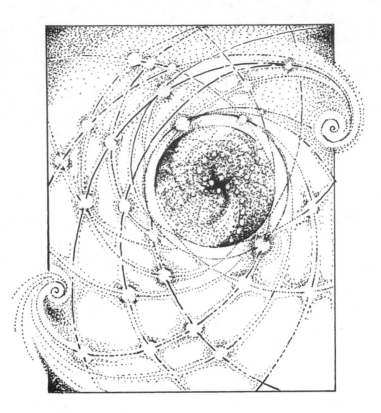

Then Gaia grew lonely. Observing her own beauties and the universe around her, she determined to share them. So she began to give birth.

Because she was all—male and female together—she needed no mate, although some say that she spun out a serpent lover from the last remaining chaos in the universe. Soon she was pregnant. Soon she gave birth. Offspring poured from her vast and fruitful womb.

One of Gaia's first children was Chronos, whose name means "time." Once Time was born, everything changed. Before there had been a flowing ocean of moments, yearning one into another, but suddenly events took shape. There were now beginnings—and endings. Death came into the world. And nothing was ever the same thereafter.

Gaia herself changed. Suddenly she felt something she had never felt before: a burning, a hunger. Gaia felt desire. Those creatures, her children, were wonderful creations. But now that time had made a story out of singularity, Gaia desired a companion. So she created, out of her vast and splendid body, the perfect lover. He was beautiful, radiant with light. And he was huge, covering every bit of her, able to satisfy her every desire: Uranus, the heavens, forever arching over the mounds and valleys of Gaia. From the instant she created him, Gaia loved Uranus.

From their union sprang forth many creatures, some marvelous, some monstrous. Eventually her children struggled with each other, but even then, mother Gaia loved all her little ones. So she does today, just as she continues to give birth with reckless abandon. Each spring we see the results of her fecundity as plants burst up through the softening soil. Each summer we feel the passion of her connection with Uranus, who showers her with light and water while she blossoms beneath him. Each fall we feel the power of earth's child Time as we watch the garden's narrative come to its inevitable conclusion. And then comes the apparent fruitless chaos of winter, an interlude before spring emerges again in Gaia's constant cycle.

IN GAIA'S NAME

In ancient times, Gaia was worshiped with barley cakes and honey—her own creations, returned to her as sacred offerings. In response, Gaia spoke to her oracular priestesses through fissures in the earth. Her messages told Gaia's people how to live—how to make choices that nourished both themselves and the earth. The Greeks celebrated their connection with the goddess in great public festivals as well as in private rituals honoring the fruitful maternity of the first and most powerful cosmic goddess.

The great oracles of Gaia stand silent now, and her festivals have long since ceased. Yet she speaks in the silent voice of inspiration to every gardener willing to hear. Like the murmur of a breeze or the gentle tapping of branches, her voice rises from the garden. Even in apparent silence, she speaks in the hum of insects fertilizing her many blooms. And what messages does she sing so softly—what oracles does she whisper into our waiting ears?

You know the answer, for she has spoken to you. You have heard her as you stood in the dawn garden, watching the dew glisten on the bright spring leaves. You have known her presence in the bright day as you stooped toward her brown skin. You have heard her in the evening as you stood beneath a fragrant night-flowering vine, its essence mingling with your own.

Gaia's message is heard with the whole being, with body, mind, and spirit. Words alone cannot capture her demand that we integrate ourselves and become integrated with her. Yet we understand her message as we move in archetypal gardening gestures: planting, cultivating, harvesting, planting again.

Magical gardeners are the last remaining oracles of the earth. Through us—through you—Gaia speaks her powerful, wordless messages. As you garden, let her sing through you; testify with your actions to her grand power. For there is nothing more important that you can do.

Appendix 1
Plant Suppliers

This selective list of providers is offered to those interested in rare or unusual, non-GMO (genetically modified), and open-pollinated or heritage plant varieties. Many other companies provide seeds and live plants, ranging from national chains to local gardening centers. These typically offer standard varieties, which may not provide sufficient depth for your needs. Some of the providers in this list specialize in a particular plant, such as the daylily, while others concentrate on plants that thrive under certain conditions, such as in shade or rainy climates. Many have print as well as online catalogs. If you order print catalogs, do the earth a favor by recycling them or shredding them into garden mulch when you're done with them.

Start by learning your gardening zone. If you don't know it already, find it at http://www.arborday.org/treeinfo/zonelookup.cfm. For best results, order from a provider in your gardening zone. Many nurseries listed have display gardens where you can see the plants and their requirements, and get ideas for your own special garden.

Ain't I Pretty Daylilies, 2915 Tobias Rd., Alcolu, SC 29001
http://daylilyflower.com

Alchemy Works Seeds for Magic, 643 Newtown St., Elmira, NY 14904
http://www.alchemy-works.com

Ambergate Gardens, 8730 County Rd. 43, Chaska, MN 55318-9358
http://www.ambergategardens.com

Amethyst Hill Nursery, 6543 South Zimmerman Rd., Aurora, OR 97002
http://amethyst-hill.com

Antique Rose Emporium (display gardens in Brenham and San Antonio, TX)
http://www.antiqueroseemporium.com

Arbor Day Foundation, 100 Arbor Ave., Nebraska City, NE 68410
http://www.arborday.org

B & D Lilies, 330 P St., Port Townsend, WA 98368
http://www.bdlilies.com

Bamboo Garden, 18900 NW Collins Rd., North Plains, OR 97133
http://www.bamboogarden.com

Big Dipper Farm, 26130 SE Green Valley Rd., Black Diamond, WA 98010
http://www.bigdipperfarm.com

Bloomingfields Farm, PO Box 5, Gaylordsville, CT 06755-0005
http://www.bloomingfieldsfarm.com

Bluestone Perennials, 7211 Middle Ridge Rd., Madison, OH 44057
http://www.bluestoneperennials.com

Breck's, PO Box 65, Guilford, IN 47022-0065
http://brecks.com

Brent and Becky's Bulbs, 7900 Daffodil Lane, Gloucester, VA 23061
http://www.brentandbeckysbulbs.com

Carlson's Gardens, PO Box 305, South Salem, NY 10590
http://www.carlsonsgardens.com

Comstock Seed, 917 Hwy. 88, Gardnerville, NV 89460
http://www.comstockseed.com

Cricket Hill Garden, 670 Walnut Hill Rd., Thomaston, CT 06787
http://www.treepeony.com

David Austin Roses, 15059 State Hwy. 64 West, Tyler, TX 75704
http://www.davidaustinroses.com

Daylily and Hosta Gardens, 2396 Roper Mountain Rd.,
Simpsonville, SC 29681
http://www.daylilyandhostagardens.com/index.html

Daylily Dreams & Hosta Haven, 27458 Covered Bridge Trail,
Harbeson, DE 19951
http://www.daylilydream.com

Denali Seed Company, 12101 Division St., Anchorage, AK 99511
http://www.denaliseed.com

Digging Dog Nursery, 31101 Middle Ridge Rd., Albion, CA 95410
http://www.diggingdog.com

E and B Farm, 541 J. C. Sullivan Rd., Louisville, MS 39339
http://www.eandbfarm.com

Easy to Grow Bulbs, 2521-A Oceanside Blvd., Oceanside, CA 92054
http://www.easytogrowbulbs.com

Evergreen Plant Nursery, 15026 Rhea County Hwy., Evensville, TN 37332
http://www.evergreenplantnursery.com

Fedco Seeds, PO Box 520, Waterville, ME 04903
http://www.fedcoseeds.com

Flower Factory, 4062 County Rd. A, Stoughton, WI 53589
http://www.theflowerfactorynursery.com

Flower Seeds Online
http://www.flowerseedsonline.org

Forest Farm, 990 Tetherow Rd., Williams, OR 97544-9599
http://www.forestfarm.com

Full Bloom Farm Peonies, 2330 Tuttle Lane, Lummi Island, WA 98262
http://www.fullbloomfarmpeonies.com

Garden Crossings, 4902 96th Ave., Zeeland, MI 49464
http://www.gardencrossings.com

Garden Perennials, 85261 Hwy. 15, Wayne, NE 68787-9801
http://www.gardenperennials.net

Great Garden Plants, PO Box 1511, Holland, MI 49424-1511
http://www.greatgardenplants.com

Green Mountain Hosta Nursery, PO Box 97, East Dover, VT 05341
https://www.greenmountainhosta.com

Greer Gardens, 1280 Goodpasture Island Rd., Eugene, OR 97401-1794
http://www.greergardens.com

Gurney's Seed & Nursery Co., PO Box 4178, Greendale, IN 47025-4178
http://www.gurneys.com

Heirloom Roses, 24062 NE Riverside Dr., St. Paul, OR 97137
http://www.heirloomroses.com

Heronswood Nursery, 300 Park Ave., Warminster, PA 18974-4818
http://www.heronswood.com

High Country Gardens, 2902 Rufina St., Santa Fe, NM 87507
http://www.highcountrygardens.com

High Mowing Organic Seeds, 76 Quarry Rd., Wolcott, VT 05680
http://www.highmowingseeds.com

Holland Bulb Farm, 8480 North 87th St., Milwaukee, WI 53224
http://www.hollandbulbfarms.com

Homestead Farm Nurseries, 3701 Hwy. EE, Owensville, MO 65066
http://www.homesteadfarms.com

Horizon Herbs, PO Box 69, Williams, OR 97544
http://www.horizonherbs.com

Hostas Direct, 19 Mid Oaks Rd., Roseville, MN 55113
http://www.hostasdirect.com

J. L. Hudson, Seedsman, Box 337, La Honda, CA 94020-0337
http://www.jlhudsonseeds.net

John Scheepers, Inc., 23 Tulip Dr., Bantam, CT 06750
http://www.johnscheepers.com

Johnny's Selected Seeds, 184 Foss Hill Rd., Albion, ME 04910
http://www.johnnyseeds.com

Joy Creek Nursery, 20300 NW Watson Rd., Scappoose, OR 97056
http://www.joycreek.com

Landreth Seed Co., 60 East High St., Bldg. #4, New Freedom, PA 17349
http://www.landrethseeds.com

Lily Garden, 4902 NE 147th Ave., Vancouver, WA 98682-6067
http://www.thelilygarden.com

Marietta Daylily Gardens, 8577 NC Hwy. 904, Fairmont, NC 28340
http://www.mariettagardens.com

Miller Nursery, 5155 NW 57th Ave., Johnston, IA 50131
http://www.millernursery.com

Mitsch Novelty Daffodils, PO Box 218, Hubbard, OR 97032
http://www.mitschdaffodils.com

Mountainview Tree Farm, 931 St. Rte. 88, Gardnerville, NV 89460
http://www.mountainviewtreefarm.com

Musser Forests Inc., 1880 Rte. 119 Hwy. North, Indiana, PA 15701-0340
http://www.musserforests.com

Natural Garden, 38W443 Hwy. 46, St. Charles, IL 60175
http://www.thenaturalgardeninc.com

Natural Gardener, 8648 Old Bee Cave Rd., Austin, TX 78735
http://www.naturalgardeneraustin.com

Netherland Bulb Co., 13 McFadden Rd., Easton, PA 18045-7819
http://www.netherlandbulb.com

Next Harvest/Seedman
http://www.nextharvest.com
http://www.seedman.com

Oakes Daylilies, 8153 Monday Rd., Corryton, TN 37721
http://www.oakesdaylilies.com

Ohio Heirloom Seeds, 277 Deer Meadow Dr., Gahanna, OH 43230
http://www.ohioheirloomseeds.com

Paradise Garden, PO Box 267, Corryton, TN 37721-0267
http://www.paradisegarden.com

Pender Nursery, PO Box 155, 2620 Wall's Store Rd., Garner, NC 27529
http://www.pendernursery.com

Pendulous Plants, PO Box 814, Horse Shoe, NC 28742
http://www.pendulousplants.com

Plant Delights Nursery, Inc., 9241 Sauls Rd., Raleigh, NC 27603
http://www.plantdelights.com

Planter's Palette, 28W571 Roosevelt Rd., Winfield, IL 60190
http://www.planterspalette.com

Quarles Daylilies, 159 Hickory Ridge Rd., Waddy, KY 40076
http://quarlesdaylilies.com

Raintree Nursery, 391 Butts Rd., Morton, WA 98356
http://www.raintreenursery.com

Rogue Valley Roses, PO Box 116, Phoenix, OR 97535
http://www.roguevalleyroses.com

Sandy Mush Herb Nursery, 316 Surrett Cove Rd., Leicester, NC 28748-5517
http://www.sandymushherbs.com

Schmid Gardens, 847 Westwood Blvd., Jackson, MI 49203
http://www.schmidgardens.com

Schreiner's Iris Gardens, 3625 Quinaby Rd. NE, Salem, OR 97303
http://www.schreinersgardens.com

Seed Savers Exchange, 3094 North Winn Rd., Decorah, IA 52101
http://www.seedsavers.org

Shady Oaks Nursery, 1601 5th St SE, PO Box 708, Waseca, MN 56093
http://www.shadyoaks.com

Siskiyou Rare Plant Nursery, 2115 Talent Ave., Talent, OR 97540
http://siskiyourareplantnursery.com

Smokey's Gardens, 101 Old Smokey Ave., Ashley, IN 46705
http://www.dayliliesforsale.com

Song Sparrow Perennial Farm, 13101 East Rye Rd., Avalon, WI 53505
http://www.songsparrow.com

Star Seed, Inc., PO Box 228, 101 Industrial Ave., Osborne, KS 67473
  http://gostarseed.com

Sterrett Gardens, PO Box 85, Craddocksville, VA 23341
  http://sterrettgardens.com

Sun Valley Garden Center, 1234 Andersen Rd., Eden Prairie, MN 44312
  http://www.qscaping.com/NetPS-Engine.asp?20000011

Sunlight Gardens, 174 Golden Lane, Andersonville, TN 37705
  http://www.sunlightgardens.com

Sunny Border Nurseries, 1709 Kensington Rd., PO Box 483,
  Kensington, CT 06037
  http://www.sunnyborder.com

Tranquil Lake Nursery, 45 River St., Rehoboth, MA 02769-1395
  http://www.tranquil-lake.com/index.htm

Twombly Nursery, 163 Barn Hill Rd., Monroe, CT 06468
  http://www.twomblynursery.com

Van Veen Nursery, 4201 SE Franklin, PO Box 86424, Portland OR 97286-0424
  http://www.vanveennursery.com

Variegated Foliage, 245 Westford Rd., Eastford, CT 06242
  http://www.variegatedfoliage.com

Wave Crest Nursery, 2509 Lakeshore Dr., Fennville, MI 49408
  http://www.wavecrestnursery.com

Wayside Gardens, One Garden Lane, Hodges, SC 29695
  http://www.waysidegardens.com

Western Native Seed, PO Box 188, Coaldale, CO 81222
  http://westernnativeseed.com

Weston Nurseries, 93 East Main St., Hopkinton, MA 01748
http://www.westonnurseries.com

White Flower Farm, PO Box 50, Litchfield, CT 06759-0050
http://www.whiteflowerfarm.com

Wildseed Farms, 100 Legacy Dr., Fredericksburg, TX 78624
http://www.wildseedfarms.com

Wildwood Farm, 10300 Sonoma Hwy., Kenwood, CA 95452
http://www.wildwoodmaples.com

Willis Orchard Company, PO Box 119, Berlin, GA 31722
http://www.willisorchards.com

Appendix 2
Garden Ornament Suppliers

One of the best places to look for tasteful garden ornaments, ranging from wind chimes to statuary to flags, is your local botanical garden. Many botanical gardens are important locations for horticultural research, and you will save yourself many failed plantings if you visit them to see what grows where *before* you start your garden project. In addition, most have gift shops that specialize in garden-related items. Consider becoming a member! Many botanical gardens have exchange programs with gardens in other locations, and touring gardens as you travel on business or pleasure can be inspirational as well as relaxing.

Museums, large and small, are also good locations for searching out ornaments for your garden. Be careful, however, to thoroughly waterproof your treasures and to move them indoors in inclement weather and, in many areas, during the winter.

The list below offers several additional options for seeking out decorations for your garden:

Ancient Wisdoms, PO Box 535, St. Clair Shores, MI 48080
    http://www.ancient-wisdoms.com

Design Toscano, Inc., 17 East Campbell St., Arlington Heights, IL 60005
    http://www.designtoscano.com

Garden Accents, 4 Union Hill Rd., West Conshohocken, PA 19428
    http://www.gardenaccents.com

The Pyramid Collection, Altid Park, PO Box 3333, Chelmsford, MA 01824
    http://www.pyramidcollection.com

Statue.com, 100 North Main St., Edwardsville, IL 62025
    http://www.statue.com

Stone Forest, 213 South St. Francis Dr., Santa Fe, NM 87501
    http://www.stoneforest.com

Appendix 3
Bibliography and Sources

Sources for Myths

Burton, John W. "'The Moon Is a Sheep': A Feminine Principle in Atuot Cosmology." *Man*, New Series, Vol. 16, No. 3 (Sept. 1981).

Evans-Pritchard, E. E. *Nuer Religion*. Oxford: Clarendon Press, 1956.

Knappert, Jan, trans. *Bantu Myths and Other Tales*. Leiden: E. J. Brill, 1977.

Lienhardt, Godfrey. *Divinity and Experience: The Religion of the Dinka*. Oxford: Clarendon Press, 1961.

Sources for Prayers

Prayers in this book are translations or interpretations of poems and songs from the following sources:

Aeschylus. *The Suppliants*.
http://www.gutenberg.org/ebooks/8714

Getty, Adele. *Goddess: Mother of Living Nature*. London: Thames & Hudson, 1990.

Gordon, R. K. *Anglo-Saxon Poetry*. Everyman's Library #794. London: M. Dent & Sons, Ltd., 1962.

Graves, Robert. *The White Goddess: A Historical Grammar of Poetic Myth*. New York: Farrar, Straus and Giroux, 1966.

Sargent, Thema, trans. *The Homeric Hymns*. New York: W. W. Norton, 1975.

Appendix 4
Garden Inspirations

Botanical Gardens in the United States

http://en.wikipedia.org/wiki/List_of_botanical_gardens_in_the_United_States

Botanical Gardens in Canada

http://en.wikipedia.org/wiki/List_of_botanical_gardens_in_Canada

Botanical Gardens Throughout the World

http://en.wikipedia.org/wiki/List_of_botanical_gardens

Atlanta Goddess Garden:
   http://www.goddessgardenatlanta.com/index.html

Botanic Gardens Conservation International:
   http://www.bgci.org

Brigit's Garden, Ireland:
   http://www.brigitsgarden.ie

Califia Garden, California:
   http://queencalifia.org

Eden Project, England:
   http://www.edenproject.com

Labyrinth Garden, Los Angeles:
   http://www.peacelabyrinth.org/

Sacred Orisha Gardens, Florida:
   http://www.ifafoundation.org/the-sacred-gardens

Tarot Garden, Italy:
   http://www.nikidesaintphalle.com

Appendix 5
Index

banana soup, 59, 62

Bast, 129–131, 133

Bast's Cat Garden, 129–130, 133

Beltane, 75–76, 81, 102

birch, xxii, 29

bleeding hearts, 108, 111, 117, 119

Bloudewedd, 1

brainstorming, 91–92

Brussels sprouts, xxiii

Caesar, Julius, 81

Camelot, 135–141

campion, 198

Candlemas (Imbolc), 75, 86, 88, 102

Cat goddess—see Bast

Catherine wheel, 79

catmint, 130, 133

catnip, 129–130, 133

Ceralia, 143

Ceres, 143–146, 148

chamomile, 115, 119, 131, 196, 204, 206, 209

Chanukah, 71